reclaimed

MAKING WHOLE WHAT
WAS BROKEN & BETRAYED

Small Group Leaders Guide

Stephanie Broersma

Practical Suggestions For Moving Through Grief

Through the sharing of her experiences following her husband's confession, Stephanie provides other women a companion in their own unique journey as they navigate the confusing and complex emotions surrounding infidelity. You will feel understanding as she walks with you, helping you navigate through the aftermath of unplanned pain and unending questions.

Stephanie's candid story of grief, turmoil and finding blessings in the moments, provide a glimpse of hope and healing to one of life's most difficult experiences: marital betrayal. She shares honest and raw memories of times that drew her into a closer relationship with God, and called upon her to search deep within to find stability during the initial period of shock and disbelief. Practical suggestions for moving through the grief provide encouragement from becoming stuck and immobilized. Stephanie sprinkles in humor and moments of joy she found within the weeks after confession, giving you permission to continue to live and experience happiness that balances the hard work of healing.

This hope-filled guide will meet those in the immediate aftermath of confession, as well as the woman who is months or years along in the journey and yet still searching to find further healing and freedom from the pain.

- **Christie Hunter,** *MA, R.C.C.; Co-Founder Theravive.com*

Through Grief and Pain to Whole-Hearted Healing

With authenticity and an unflinching look back on her own marriage crisis, Stephanie Broersma has crafted a Bible study guide for women who suffer betrayal by a spouse. When her own marriage was threatened by her husband's infidelity and struggles with pornography, Stephanie was shattered to discover very little guidance in Christian circles. She learned that many women in her situation suffer in silence, and that the Church is not always a supportive or safe place for women whose husbands are unfaithful.

2 Corinthians 1:4 says that God comforts us in all our troubles, so that we can comfort others with the same Godly comfort. Based on her own journey with God through grief and pain, to whole-hearted healing and restoration of her marriage, Stephanie created a ministry to help other women. This Bible study is the result of her search of Scripture to find comfort and direction, and incorporates the questions and experiences of many women who face this painful situation.

With respect for God's word and compassion for all parties involved, Stephanie guides women as they process through the natural emotions of shock, grief, self-blame, and anger, and gives them hope and positive direction for the future. Stephanie's own marriage survived, and thrived, after rising from the ashes of infidelity and shame. This study will be a comfort and encouragement to others on the journey.

- **Ramona Stumpf,** *Director of Life-Changers, North County Christ the King Community Church*

A Journey From Personal Devastation to Restoration

Stephanie Broersma has been Reclaimed! This Study Guide is a window to her soul, giving a full view of the pain, brokenness and heartache caused by betrayal in her marriage. Stephanie is vulnerable, honest and inviting in the way that she shares her journey from personal devastation to restoration. I have been honored to witness Stephanie allow God to create beauty from ashes through the power of forgiveness and grace.

Embrace her words of empathy and understanding as she identifies feelings yet unnamed in your heart. This is a must-read for anyone needing to be Reclaimed from the pain of betrayal.

~ **Kurt Langstraat,** MA; Senior Pastor, *North County Christ the King Community Church*; Lynden, Washington

From *Reclaimed Small Group* Attendees:

Reclaimed is a safe space to begin the journey of wholeness after the unthinkable has happened. Knowing that I'm not alone in the pain I've experienced has been a true comfort. The Bible-based material we studied helped me start the pathway to healing and forgiveness, and reminded me that I can trust and rely on God, who will never let me down.

- Small Group Attendee

Through this group, I've been challenged to seek Him (Jesus) first and take the focus off the hurt around me so He can call me out on everything that takes the focus off of Him. While any change can seem difficult, the reward for doing the hard work is immeasurable when it comes to deeply being challenged daily to refuse anything less than being seen as 'the daughter of the King Most High.

- Small group Attendee

Related Materials

- Reclaimed Small Group Guide
- Reclaimed: Finding Your Identity after Marital Betrayal
- Reclaimed My Blessings Journal

Thank you for your purchase of the Reclaimed Leaders Study Guide! All supplemental materials for the Reclaimed Small Group are written into the course and available upon request. Contact **stephanie@reclaimedministry.com** to request your digital file and we'll get them to you free of charge.

Reclaimed Ministry would love to help get you into the network of those leading groups around the country and pray over the preparation that goes into leading women into healing.

To skip straight to the small group materials, scroll to page 23. Prior to that is my story, which gives you context into how and why Reclaimed Ministry was developed. I'm honored to help guide you through the small group process as well, so make sure to reach out with any questions or if you're interested in Reclaimed Leadership Training.

Blessings,
Stephanie Broersma

Reclaimed Small Group Leaders Guide

A Course To Guide You Through Betrayal Within Your Marriage

By **Stephanie Broersma**

ISBN: 978-179-138-2490

Names have been changed to protect privacy.

Cover Design by Lisa DenBleyker, Lynden, WA and Chad Williams, Lynden, WA. Printed in the United States. For more information, contact:

Reclaimed Ministry
Stephanie Broersma
P.O. Box 569
Lynden, Washington, 98264
United States of America

To learn more about Reclaimed Ministry and related materials, visit:
www.reclaimedministry.com
@reclaimedministry

Table of Contents (Leader Guide):

Table of Contents (User Guide):

reclaimed

MAKING WHOLE WHAT
WAS BROKEN & BETRAYED

Dedication

To my sweet older sister, Traci, my biggest cheerleader.
I can hear you still, cheering me on from heaven.
To the women who have, and continue to trust me with their stories.
And to my husband Tim, who continues to pursue me daily.

Introduction
A Normal Girl with an Unexpected Story

*"Come and listen, all you who fear God; let me tell you
what He has done for me."*

Psalm 66:16; NIV

My childhood was quite textbook, according to what North American society standards were and how ordinary families were perceived on TV in the 1980s. I grew up in a Christian home with two parents, Paul and Cheryl, who were and still are, forty years later, dedicated to family, work, and providing stability within our home unit. The greatest gift my parents gave me was the blessing of a two-parent home. Yes, I heard and saw fights like any normal married couple has in their years together, but our home was always secure, safe, and loving.

Girl Meets Boy

Tim Broersma and I had no intention of dating in high school. That didn't stop me from admiring him. As a freshman, I thought he was so cute, I even wrote him a love letter. Oh, to be young and naïve! I'm not sure what my intentions were in writing that silly letter, but his sister Becky was my best friend and, being new to the school, I generally trusted what she had to say. She talked a lot about her brother, and when Tim finally tried to ask me out, I didn't give him the chance to complete his sentence. "No," I blurted. "Becky said to say no!" I'm so grateful for that advice.

We made our separate ways through high school. I had just graduated when our paths crossed again. This time, something sparked between us, and we began a "just friends" phase that lasted about three to four months. I worked at Goldie's Bar and Grill that summer, and to my surprise, I would often find notes, gifts, or Tim by my car, waiting for me to finish my shift. We spent many hours at the local diner Shari's, sitting over a cup of coffee or hot chocolate, discussing life, breakups, and, most often, the topic of faith.

We spent countless hours chatting the summer evenings away just as friends. It wasn't until I moved down to Seattle for college that things started to change, and the thought of being apart became unbearable.

Marriage to Honeymoon in Paris

Tim and I dated for a few years before he asked me to marry him. From the proposal to the wedding ceremony, everything was perfect. We honeymooned in Paris, then traveled to Scandinavia over our first-year anniversary with the semi-professional barbershop quartet Tim was a part of.

Time passed, and we were secure in our jobs, living comfortably in our first home. It was a fixer-upper, but it was ours. Tim's five-year plan—to hold off on children for five years—lasted all but two years, when our firstborn daughter Addison arrived. After some hard discussions, Tim and I sold our first home and moved into a rental home for two years. Tim and I worked really well together. We shared many of the responsibilities within our business and our home without fighting or arguing.

I noticed nothing out of the normal until my second pregnancy. That was in 2008, the same time we were moving to our current home. I was three months pregnant and having complications with the pregnancy.

I began to notice a distance between us—our touch and communications were off. I can count on one hand how many times we were sexually intimate during the pregnancy.

Through the duration of my pregnancy, Tim became increasingly busy with his work. My belly was growing, and the end date was near. Our little Charlie was born three weeks early via c-section. In the moments before my surgery, Tim was busy typing on his computer, while the nurse poked me five times to start the IV. I remember looking over at him, tears welling, searching for comfort.

Charlie was born with lung and breathing problems, and they kept him in the nursery for a full twenty-four hours. Because my blood pressure was extremely low, the nurses wouldn't allow me out of bed. Consequently, I was shown only pictures of my little man cub. Depression crept closer to me. When I was finally cleared to go to Charlie, other family members had already touched, smelled, and kissed his little cheeks—but I was given only five minutes to quickly visit, and then was sent back to bed. When the nurses finally brought Charlie to my room, Tim lay sleeping on the couch. He was so into his work, he even had contractors meeting him outside my hospital room. The first time Addi saw her brother, my Mom was there, not Tim.

I didn't recognize my postpartum depression until after it had passed. Neither did I notice how far away my husband was until it was too late.

By the time Charlie was six months old, the cloud of depression had lifted. At the same time, Tim was sharing an office with his business partner, Greg, and they had conversations about the book of Revelation. Tim's secret was still unknown, but something Greg said slam-dunked my husband into a breaking moment. After that conversation, Tim began feverishly searching for a scripture that would allow him to confess his sins to Jesus but not have to be completely honest with me, his wife. This search went on for six months, but in the process gave way to a new man. Tim recommitted his life to Christ, and things on the outside were changing.

I saw more engagement at home when we lay in bed and prayed. I didn't have to prod him to pray—he offered it willingly. We were reading devotions and experiencing true worship together. Our communication consistently improved—we still never yelled or fought with each other; we simply worked out issues or differences. I felt loved. I felt cherished. I trusted our relationship and the patterns we had made over seven years of marriage.

Deleted Conversations

One day, I opened a Facebook message and found deleted threads of conversation not appropriate within a marriage. I felt instant panic. Fear paralyzed me as I recognized what I was reading. It can't be, I thought. My gut told me there was more and I knew.

Tim later confessed to a ten-year pornography addiction that started back in high school. And then he confessed to extramarital affairs—yes, plural!—that took place during my second pregnancy. My spirit was crushed.

All I had was my faith in Christ—and as I looked to Him to guide me, I had no idea what the next steps toward healing would be, nor did I know how to respond the next time I saw my husband. Even as my world crumbled, I was determined to fight for us, for our marriage and I refused to allow Satan to turn our marriage into another dismal statistic.

We kept our marriage collapse extremely private until two years after Tim's confession. At that time, our church asked if we would be willing to share our testimonies via video. We did, and the response that followed was incredible. We received notes of encouragement for stepping out and sharing our story. Tim and I were asked to speak at local churches, on radio talk shows, at marriage retreats, and to share our story on national television.

The very thing that made me crawl into a fetal position and cry until I had no more tears, the thing that had offered no hope of repair—God used to bring hope to others in similar situations. I began meeting regularly with women at local coffee shops and through text messages and emails. Long phone calls spent listening, praying with women, and connecting them to the right resources in their area became frequent. And I discovered a common thread running through my communications with hurting women—they felt they had no one to go to in their own church; there was no group or resource that provided real, tangible advice and support for broken women.

People started asking why I hadn't started yet. When I was going to get a group going? I resisted at first, until a mentor challenged me by lighting a fire under my seat. "Why not?" She urged. "Write your own curriculum; get it going."

An Ugly Topic

The more I heard about the lack of support for women like me in their local churches, the more frustrated I grew. Some women were told, "Be quiet; it's your fault your husband went elsewhere." Others were told, "Don't say anything to anyone. It's not pornography unless it's in front of a computer." This was appalling! The need to educate and encourage women on their journey toward healing became so evident to me that I had no choice but to act.

God made it very clear to me during the months of healing and reconstruction that followed Tim's betrayal, what my future purpose would be in life. It is now my heart's passion to speak out about my darkest days and to share the hope God offered in my brokenness, during the worst time of my life.

My prayer is that you will see in this 30 Day Personal Journal the same divine web that held me up when my two feet were too weak to stand and that you will find the same hope I experienced through the cross of Christ. Nothing is too messy or too far gone that God cannot restore. With Him by your side, you can deal with the pain inside and the muck outside. And you can walk with your head held high, offering God all the glory for the amazing, reclaimed story of your life.

A Daughter of the King

I am not a professional in the area of marriage and betrayal. I can't offer you "30 Easy Steps to Overcoming the Betrayal Game." I'm simply a girl with a story who dedicates herself to parenting, keeping the washing machine running, placing edible somethings on our dinner plates . . . and keeping the passion alive in our marriage. I don't have a bunch of letters that follow my name, nor do I have a degree hanging on my wall that qualifies me for this task. I don't claim to have it all together, and certainly, there are days when our home would benefit from more structure. I'm weak when it comes to sweets, still struggle with how I view myself, and will be the first to tell you if things are not okay. What I do know is this; I am a daughter of the King who loves me regardless of my weaknesses or strengths. God saw that I was capable of the task to help others, and He has given me a voice to extend hope to lives of women who are shattered from marital infidelity.

My husband cherishes me as his bride and loves me more every day. I trust in us, in who we have become together, and will stand up for our marriage any day of the week. My faith got me here today, and my faith will carry me through tomorrow. My hope for you—as a reader, leader, or broken woman—is that you will find how deeply you are loved by your Savior and that you are not alone in this moment.

How did God heal me? That's what I am going to share with you and here are some practical ways to use this book:

1. **This is your story.** I challenge you to keep the focus on your heart as you answer the Personal Reflection section in your small group and invite God into your journey with the understanding you can't change those within your sphere.

2. **Don't rush the process and become overwhelmed.** If it's too much, try answering one reflection question and choose one scripture to meditate on from the scripture section throughout the week.

3. **Put your armor on.** You are entering a spiritual battle that the enemy wants nothing more than for you to fail miserably at as you desire to reclaim truth in your life. Read the armor passage in Ephesians 6:10-18 out loud in prayer every day.

4. **Be in prayer.** Prayer is vital even on a good day. Asking a friend or mentor to cover you in prayer as you process what you are reading.

5. **Seek God's blessings.** Grab a Reclaimed Blessing Journal (info in the Resource Section) and write down the ways God is reminding you of his goodness and faithfulness. Journal your prayer requests and highlight the ways God responds to your requests. Focus on the beauty of your journey through your words. Share with those in your group!

6. **Get connected.** You may feel like you're doing this alone but that's not God's plan for life to be lived alone. Join the Reclaimed Ministry Community in a closed group on Facebook. You can find out more at www.reclaimedministry.com

Stephanie Broersma

June 2018
Lynden, Washington

"To bestow on them a crown of beauty instead of ashes, the oil of gladness instead of mourning, and a garment of praise instead of a spirit of despair. They will be called oaks of righteousness. Instead of their shame my people will receive a double portion, and instead of disgrace they will rejoice in their inheritance; and so they will inherit a double portion in their land, and everlasting joy will be theirs."

Isaiah 61:3,7

Purpose

The purpose of Reclaimed is to help women find hope and healing amidst the pain and suffering caused by betrayal in their marriages. Our hope is that God would set a fire in our hearts to become more passionate, find greater joy, and an intimacy we never thought deserved. As we dive into the Word and hold each other **accountable**, may we in **confidence** seek truth, speak out of **respect**, **protect** each others stories and always **give God the glory** for even the smallest of baby steps towards complete restoration in our hearts. I pray that you will find beauty in the pile of ashes before you and be redeemed through grace, and receive the double portion set before you.

{Reminders}

- speak out of respect for our marriages, spouses, and ourselves
- keep each others comments, questions, and stories confidential
- share with an open heart but with God's intentions in consideration
- respect each others emotions
- walk in humility, forgiveness, and with love

Our Commitment

In order to get the most out of this study, we commit to allow God to open old wounds, showing us where growth is needed, forgiveness can be spoken, and attempts at healing accepted. God is ready to do big things in our hearts and marriages if we're willing to let Him.

☙

When you reflect back to the raw moments in the betrayal of your vow, what are some of the emotions, the feelings you experienced? {betrayal, mistrust, rejection, embarrassment, shame, violation, unworthy, dirty, defeated, humiliation, angry, outraged, frustrated, dismay, crushed, deceived, dishonesty, shock}. Over the next twelve weeks, we will walk through the hurt caused by betrayal. Our focus will be on **CHOOSING** to see God in the pain, and learning to trust in God's promise for His cherished, beloved daughters as we build a body of support, encouragement, and prayer around each other.

Course Outline:

The Initial Shock & Betrayal

Betrayal, Bitterness, Shame

Navigating Grief & Exhaustion

Grief, Weariness, Image

The Choice to Forgive

Forgiveness, Hope, Trust

Educating Our Realities

Education, Communication, Support

A Restored Smile

Restoration, Redeemed, Joy

Perspective Moving Forward

Boundaries, Perspective, Dating

❧

If you have any questions, comments, needs or would like to chat a bit longer about a topic, please contact: (Make sure to give your contact information to those in attendance)

Reclaimed Ministry

P.O. Box 569

Lynden, WA 98264

stephanie@reclaimedministry.com

www.reclaimedministry.com

@reclaimedministry

Course Recommendations & Suggestions

Materials Included:

- *Reclaimed Study Guide* (Decide if you as the leader will pre-purchase the study guides or if the attendee will purchase her own study guide. Make sure you give yourself time to order and for shipment.)

After you purchase the *Reclaimed Small Group Leaders Guide* contact stephanie@reclaimedminsitry.com to receive an email with the digital file of the following print outs that make leading a group more useful.

- Reclaimed Introduction Information Card
- Reclaimed Ministry LOGO for advertising use
- 2 printed articles (*When A Spouse Is Unfaithful* by Tim Jackson, *When Forgiveness Seems Impossible* by Tim Jackson)
- Reclaimed Spiritual Inventory
- Who I Am In Christ
- Forgiveness Bookmark
- SOAP Handout
- Three Trees Diagram
- 4 Responses
- Lies You Believe Postcard
- Trauma Prayer

Additional Suggestions: Having a large bin to gather and store your weekly supplies allows you keep things in one place.

- pens
- pocket folders to collect print outs
- tissue boxes
- name tags
- roll of duct tape
- building blocks
- yard clippers
- large nails with purple ribbon
- water bottles

A note about the content:

While the content is developed to spur individual growth, it's also structured in a way to promote corporate growth amongst the women in attendance. As the course progresses, the content decreases, leaving room for more conversation and discussion. Generally the group starts in a more quiet and reserved manner, but as the women share, open up, and develop bonds, the conversation and sharing will increase. Don't feel tied to accomplishing each section in one week, as the most important aspect of the course is the topical discussions that occur around the content for the week. If the session has to go long, or continue the following week, that's ok! The average length to complete the Reclaimed curriculum is twelve weeks. Expect those in attendance to continue some form of communication with their leader post group. There have been groups that continue to meet once a month staying connected with each other and reviewing the content within the course or to continue previous discussions.

Before the first meeting:

- Gather all material (pre-purchased Study Guides and materials found on the website link) and organize in a folder making it easy to hand out on the guided week.

- The day before you meet with the Reclaimed Small Group, gather the email addresses from those women interested in attending and send out an email with all addresses blind copied. I say blind copied for the sole purpose that most women who will be in attendance will be terrified sharing their stories; some have never shared in a group setting before. Some come from violent relationships and live in fear of a spouse finding out about them attending and returning home only to receive backlash. Most women believe they are alone in this situation, even though they realize others share similar stories. Many are afraid of judgement if other women find out they don't have their marriage all together. Only after the first meeting, after you've had a chance to get permission from those attending, would I suggest disclosing personal email addresses.

- Here is a suggested first email: (More example emails are in the very back of your leaders guide including suggested post meeting emails. Feel free to copy or write your own.)

Subject: The Initial Shock & Betrayal

Time: Monday, 6:30pm

Location: Life Changers Front Room (Westside of the church building)

I am excited to see God move in our hearts and minds as we seek His healing through Reclaimed! Know that myself and others will, and are, praying for you as we talk about some of the deepest hurts in our lives.

We are just a day away from beginning our study on finding hope in the midst of betrayal. I wanted to give you a heads up, and will continue to do so prior to each week, on the topic that will be discussed. Included will be a glimpse into women's journals, a few discussion questions and scriptures to review. Start thinking about the topic and review the questions and scriptures to prepare your heart for the group.

It has been 9 years since that fateful evening of confession in my marriage. God has been so good and has done miracles in my marriage. I'm still on a path of healing and may not have all the answers, but do know that we serve a God who loves us, who desires us to find healing and wants to bless us with JOY! This study was born out of a story of hope and restoration.

Praying God will fill the voids in your life and you will feel His love in your heart!

An excerpt from "a broken wife's journal"....

"Something inside me immediately died. I could not believe what I just heard. This could not be real. I thought I had married a believer!! After all, he went to a Christian school, grew up in a CRC church, and <u>*professed*</u> *to be a believer!! Who was THIS person? How could this be?? I had chosen all the right qualifications in a partner!! You see, I had grown up in an environment where affairs and divorces simply did not happen. My family put Christ at the head of all that we did, and Satan stayed away!! I didn't have the background or landscape of this environment to even imagine it* <u>*could*</u> *happen. His words completely leveled me.*

But somehow, I needed to be at my new job in an hour, so I numbly went into an 'out of body' experience, and somehow functioned as if nothing had just destroyed my world. No one could know!! I am not sure how I got through that day, but I did. Once I got home, I became sick to my stomach and the migraine hit. All I could do was go to bed and cry out to God....."HOW COULD THIS BE"!! Hadn't I been doing all the right things for YOU, my husband, my children, living my life for YOU!! We had the marriage I thought my husband wanted, trying to please him in every way. Never would I have suspected this. How could I have missed it? I felt like such a fool. How could I be so stupid? Whats wrong with me?

I felt so degraded, and even embarrassed! I must really be an awful, terrible, unattractive woman that he would want to leave me. The ugly negative humiliating feelings bombarded me and refused to stop. I would never be happy again. My marriage as I knew it was violated and over, and what was once ours, was no longer."

Discussion Questions to prepare to discuss at this week's group:

- When you are faced with a trigger, how do you respond and communicate your worries with your spouse?
- When you reflect back to the raw moments in the betrayal of your vow, what are some of the emotions, the feelings you experienced?

- Have you shared your story with anyone? What prevents you from sharing?

Scriptures to review prior to this week's group:
- Romans 12:17-21
- John 18
- Proverbs 14:10
- 1 John 1:9
- Genesis 3:10
- Psalm 34:4-5

Blessings,
Stephanie Broersma
www.reclaimedministry.com

How to prepare for the first meeting: Suggested ways to set up your space of gathering

- Whether you are meeting around a table, on comfy couches or in a circle with chairs, make it inviting and comfortable for the women attending. Make the space warm and inviting. You may have "runners" before the meeting even begins, or shortly after, so make it a safe environment that causes the women to relax. **A few suggestions: 1.)** Have a little treat or snack for the women to snack on, i.e. Jelly Bellies provide a fidget snack that creates no mess, most women love them and gives you a conversation starter about a favorite flavor. **2.)** Having multiple tissues boxes near seats so they are easily accessible to those in need. This can be a very stressful study for some. **3.)** Consider an oil diffuser with calming scents to fill the room. Creating the most comfortable and safe environment will best ensure the most successful outcome for your small group. **4.)** If your meeting space has other foot traffic right outside the door, consider a radio with praise and worship music outside of your meeting space to create white noise to muffle the conversation.
- Place a workbook on each seat prior to the women arrival. If you choose to have the women purchase their own, send out a reminder email two weeks prior to purchase their own workbook. You may want to have a few on hand for backup.
- Place a Reclaimed Information Card on top of each workbook or seat and have each women fill it out before your small group begins.
- Reclaimed has a list of suggested books to read in the back of the study guide as well on the website. If possible, have a few each week laid out to review, read the back cover or make reference to during your meeting. Feel free to add your own.

Betrayal

Leader Sharing: *A Whisper From God* was a prayer one of Stephanie's Go-To friends wrote to her in those first few weeks after confession. It continues to speak peace to those she shares it with and gives many permission to just rest in God's truth. Begin your first meeting with a word of prayer; feel free to use this one as a suggestion. It is listed in the study guide for those attending small group.

A whisper from God...

"My dear sweet child, I know your pain. right now I want you to know I am here with you in that pain. As you struggle to breathe, remember I am the breath of your life. I breathe new life into you. I control the wind and the water. I am in control of your situation. I have not left you alone - I am here with you.

Take my comfort and wrap it around you like a blanket giving you warmth. Turn to me even though you may feel I am far away. I am here with you. Let me take your pain and heal you. Let me take your pain and make you stronger. Draw near to me and I will give you My strength. Let me be all you need right now. Give it all to me and I will take your pain and give you my peace.

Because I love you more than anything - I AM HERE FOR YOU..." [1]

The book *The Myth of the Greener Grass* by J. Allan Petersen, has a great illustration of what some of us may be feeling right now. It goes like this...

"A little boy was asked by his father to say grace at the table. While the rest of the family watched, the little guy eyed every dish of food his mother had prepared. After the examination he bowed his head and honestly prayed, "Lord, I don't like the looks of it, but I thank you for it and I'll eat it anyway. Amen." [2]

Leader Sharing: We've been served a dish of betrayal and whether we like it or not, we must face it. Begin by sharing your personal story of betrayal in 2-3 minutes realizing that there is limited time to share all the details within your story. Ask others to do the same. This will take some time depending on the size of your group. Don't rush this process. The first step in healing is accepting that we have a wound that needs healing. Over the course of the next few weeks, much more of our stories will be revealed.

This is not a time to disclose all the details of intimate conversations or the details within the discovery or confession. This first sharing is to orient all in attendance with each other's story, as everyone's betrayal looks different; whether it be through addiction, emotional or physical affairs. This open sharing time, helps break down walls of fear, and lays the foundation for the transparency required to ensure a successful course.

A side note: Remind the women that in sharing during your meeting today, and throughout the rest of the small group, we may talk about our spouse, but always out of respect, regardless of how they hurt you. This is not a place to husband bash or shame. It's important that the leader reflects this priority in all her times of sharing.

"A little lie is like a little pregnancy - it doesn't take long before everyone knows."
- C.S. Lewis

"Every lie creates distance between relationships."
- David Powlison

When you are at your <u>weakest</u> point, your only other option is to <u>rely</u> on God.

No betrayal looks the same and can sneak up on a person through gossip, lies, actions or the lack of engagement. Since Adam and Eve betrayed God, and allowed sin to enter our world, betrayal has been almost unavoidable as one of the primary delivery mechanisms for sin. You may be thinking, "I'll never get over it. What happened to me was so wrong. It hurt so much. I've been scarred so deeply by betrayal and brutality. My anger rages like a nuclear furnace inside me. It seems as permanent, as destructive, and as deep as the hurt."

The Bible is full of examples of betrayal:

• Jesus was betrayed. Judas betrayed Jesus after years of sharing meals, talking, praying and laughing together. **Psalm 41:9** *"Even my close friend, whom I trusted, he who shared my bread, has lifted up his heel against me."*

• We read in **Isaiah 53:3,** *"He was despised and rejected by men, a man of sorrows, and familiar with suffering."*

• **John 13:2,** *"Jesus was troubled in spirit and testified, "I tell you the truth, one of you is going to betray me."*

• Absalom betrayed his father David. **(2 Samuel 15-19)**

Those closest to Jesus were the ones that hurt Him the most. Sometimes physical pain is less painful than the words spoken against you. I would imagine that when the rooster cried three times over, the betrayal Jesus experienced is much like the pain a wife experiences in the midst of betrayal within her vow. Jesus knows our pains. He became man and understands our hurts, anxieties, and our deepest flesh wounds. There is nothing Jesus doesn't understand, and He is waiting to be your Friend in the darkness.

Betrayal is ugly. If you ignore it, like a weed it will corrupt your foundation and cause bitterness to tear your life apart. Don't allow the pain to determine your tomorrow. God's Word is truth and it will fertilize your soul, remove your bitterness, and bring light to the darkness.

Part of healing is being able to see past the betrayal and allow it to bond you closer to your spouse. This is not a fast food fix; there is no easy fix to heal the pain from betrayal. God challenges us to crucify the flesh and turn the other cheek.

Leader Emphasis: Share how we aren't to stay stuck in the muck. God desires for us to look upward and move forward with Him as we navigate these emotions.

Betrayal becomes the HEAT to our situation. (see Three Trees Diagram) The situation does not **make** us who we are. The situation **reveals** who we are.

Leader Sharing: The Three Trees diagram allows us to locate the source of pain. It's much like a road map to our emotions. The heat is the source of pain which cause revolving good consequences and revolving bad consequences; both result in either good fruit or bad fruit. We will expand more on this throughout our study. Much like accepting our situation of betrayal, the heat shows us the source of our pain.

Tim Jackson writes for the ministry now is recognized as Our Daily Bread. Here is a little of what his article "When A Spouse Is Unfaithful" has to say which can be found in the back of your binder.

"No words adequately describe the trauma a person suffers when a spouse's affair is exposed. Many report that it is the most dreadful thing they have ever faced - more excruciating than losing a parent, being diagnosed with cancer, or being fired.

An affair infects a vicious wound to the heart of a faithful spouse. Wounded spouses often feel, "While I may look the same on the outside, inside I'm hemorrhaging and I can't stop it." Most betrayed spouses feel as if they are going crazy - especially during the initial stages of shock.

Gone is the sense of being intact and whole. Self-respect is shattered and those betrayed commonly ask themselves, " Why didn't I speak up earlier when I sensed something was wrong?"

Betrayal can strip the heart of any sense of constancy, security, and meaning. Feelings of being used, discarded, and rejected replace feelings of being chosen, special, and valued." [3]

<u>Questions for Discussion and Reflection:</u>
- Are you able to locate the heat in your life? How do you see God when the pressure is on and the heat of the situation is overwhelming? What do you run to?

Leader Sharing: (example of one leaders sharing - insert your own or use as a guide to discussion)

"The HEAT in my life was my husbands confession. At the very darkest hour in our marriage, God spoke to me saying, "It is well." It was as if God took over my physical actions for the next hour until I could touch the ground again. It was even a challenge to put my shoes on and walk to the kitchen; my body felt robbed of doing the simplest things due to the shock in Tim's confession. I ran to church and found close support with family and friends. Unfortunately, some have had extremely destructive behaviors upon discovery or confession; retaliation affairs, spending sprees or causing physical harm to themselves or others."

- In your moment of shock, did you hear God's still small voice? If not, do you think He wasn't there? Do you feel betrayal from God?

- When you are faced with a trigger, how do you respond and communicate your worries with your spouse? If the marriage ended in divorce, how have you been able to deal with triggers? What are your buttons?

Leader Sharing: (example of one leaders sharing)
"I ask how Tim's eyes are, how his mind is doing. I pray and ask God to remove the fear and stomp out the lies. I ask Tim to pray for me and tell him I'm struggling. Inviting others in to pray with me has removed the weight of the burden/trigger. What are your thoughts, words, actions, emotions, choices? For some divorced women, seeing other couples can trigger negative emotions."

Betrayal puts a fog over your judgment in relationships. It clouds your vision to respond and react in a trusting manner.

- Betrayal looks different to everyone. How did/does it look like to you? Are you a vengeance-taker or are you transformed to do courageous good in the face of evil?

Leader Sharing: (example)
"My betrayal was lonely, terrifying, real and extremely painful. I felt isolated. It sucked the air out of me. The betrayal and path of sin completely blindsided me - I couldn't find my footing. It paralyzed me. It destroyed my ability to parent or to simply see myself as worthy of anything good."

- How did God face betrayal and overcome the doubts of believers and followers?

Leader Sharing: Challenge your group to look at these verses to see how Jesus dealt with betrayal.
John 18:1, Matthew 26:30, Luke 22:42

What Does the Bible Say?

- **Proverbs 25:9,** "If you argue your case with a neighbor, do not betray another man's confidence."

- **2 Chronicles 26:16,** "But after Uzziah became powerful, his pride led to his downfall. He was unfaithful to the Lord his God."

Leader Reading and Emphasis: Matthew Henry's Concise Commentary says: The transgression of the kings before Uzziah was, forsaking the temple of the Lord, and burning incense upon idolatrous altars. But his transgression was going into the holy place, and attempting to burn incense upon the altar of God. See how hard it is to avoid one extreme, and not run into another. Pride of heart was at the bottom of his sin; a lust that ruins many. Instead of lifting up the name of God in gratitude to him who had done so much for him, his heart was lifted up to his hurt.

Pride was at the bottom of his transgression, and thus God humbled him, and put dishonor upon him. Those that covet forbidden honors, forfeit allowed ones. Adam, being caught at the tree of knowledge which he may not eat of, denied himself of the tree of life which he may have eaten of. [4]

Pride more often than not, is the fuel that starts the flame of an affair.

- **Luke 22:54-62,** "Then seizing him, they led him away and took him into the house of the high priest. Peter followed at a distance. And when some there had kindled a fire in the middle of the courtyard and had sat down together, Peter sat down with them. A servant girl saw him seated there in the firelight. She looked closely at him and said, "This man was with him." But he denied it. "Woman, I don't know him," he said. A little later someone else saw him and said, "You also are one of them." "Man, I am not!" Peter replied. About an hour later another asserted, "Certainly this fellow was with him, for he is a Galilean." Peter replied, "Man, I don't know what you're talking about!" Just as he was speaking, the rooster crowed. The Lord turned and looked straight at Peter. Then Peter remembered the word the Lord had spoken to him: "Before the rooster crows today, you will disown me three times." And he went outside and wept bitterly."

- **Psalm 41:9**, "Even my close friend, someone I trusted, one who shared my bread, has turned against me."

- **Deuteronomy 32:15**, "Jeshurun grew fat and kicked; filled with food, they became heavy and sleek. They abandoned the God who made them and rejected the Rock their Savior."

Leader Reading and Emphasis: Nelson's Bible Commentary: "Since the nation had received God's revelation and His instruction, it should have become upright (vs.4). Instead, the nation would grow fat and rebel." Doesn't this match our lives, and the growth of pride we experience? [5]

- **Proverbs 27:6**, "Wounds from a friend can be trusted, but an enemy multiplies kisses."

Leader Suggestion: Read John 18 as a group, and discuss it's application to your discussion.

- **Matthew 5:9-11**, "Blessed are the peacemakers, for they will be called children of God. Blessed are those who are persecuted because of righteousness, for theirs is the kingdom of heaven. Blessed are you when people insult you, persecute you and falsely say all kinds of evil against you because of me."

- **Matthew 5:38-48**, "You have heard that it was said, 'Eye for eye, and tooth for tooth.' But I tell you, do not resist an evil person. If anyone slaps you on the right cheek, turn to them the other cheek also. And if anyone wants to sue you and take your shirt, hand over your coat as well. If anyone forces you to go one mile, go with them two miles. Give to the one who asks you, and do not turn away from the one who wants to borrow from you. You have heard that it was said, 'Love your neighbor and hate your enemy.' But I tell you, love your enemies and pray for those who persecute you, that you may be children of your Father in heaven. He causes his sun to rise on the evil and the good, and sends rain on the righteous and the unrighteous. If you love those who love you, what reward will you get? Are not even the tax collectors doing that? And if you greet only your own people, what are you doing more than others? Do not even pagans do that? Be perfect, therefore, as your heavenly Father is perfect."

- **Lamentations 1:3,19**, "After affliction and harsh labor, Judah has gone into exile. She dwells among the nations; she finds no resting place. All who pursue her have overtaken her in the midst of her distress. I called to my allies but they betrayed me. My priests and my elders perished in the city while they searched for food to keep themselves alive."

These verses are talking about the betrayal of the nation and the people who should have been of help were they themselves in trouble. Nelson's Compact Bible Commentary says: "The book of Lamentations reveals the broken heart of the prophet Jeremiah over the national tragedy that had unfolded before his eyes; Jerusalem, God's city, had fallen to the Babylonians. The people of Israel had chosen to reject God. Yet even in this time of suffering there was hope. The Lord would not discipline His people forever; He would eventually restore those who waited on Him.

The scriptures tackle some of the toughest questions faced by God's people: How can God's love and justice be reconciled with our pain? If God is in control of history, how can a nation suffer so much? Where was God during His people's unhappiest hour? The anger of God is a sign that He cares. The Lord's anger is never unreasonable. Even in His display of anger, God is still full of mercy and grace. His faithfulness is the greatest comfort to those who suffer." [6]

Leader Sharing: (Fill in with your own story if you feel comfortable.)
Betrayal weighed heavy on my body and mind that first night post confession. I felt so dirty from all the truth that I became aware of through Tim's confession; the confession dumped in my lap which was full of lust, pornography, multiple affairs and years of lies. In attempts to wash the filth of confession off of my body, I took such a hot shower and scrubbed my skin so aggressively that I made my arms bleed. Nothing I did could remove the betrayal that now seemed to define me.

Betrayal and Bitterness can cause us to hear things differently as we mix the facts with the negative opinions of those facts. With Hollywood making affairs seem like a romantic escape filled with opportunities and success, we can easily allow our minds to create a fantasy of what happened. Society has quickly accepted this attitude and places instant blame on the spouse left in shambles. Be aware of the facts so you don't fall into Satan's trap to deceive your mind and cause you to believe lies.

We are told...Fact:	**We hear...Negative Opinion:**
"My husband loves another woman."	"I'm ugly and not worthy of his love."
"I was deceived in my marriage."	"I will never be able to trust him again."
"The betrayal hurts so deeply."	"I will never forgive or be healed."

"This has never happened in my family before."   "Our reputation is destroyed."

"Our marriage has failed."   "I'm a terrible wife and mother."

Your entire thought process will become distorted and inaccurate when under stress and turmoil. Make sure you separate the facts from fantasy.

Brokenness, or despair, can be detected in tears and death, in suffering and agony, damage and decay which could result in anger or greed, selfishness or loneliness or even despair.

Bitterness

*"Forgiveness is agreeing to live with the consequences of another person's sin. You are going to live with those consequences anyway whether you like it or not, so the only choice you have is whether you will do so in the **bondage of bitterness** or in the **freedom of forgiveness**. It may seem unfair and you may wonder where the justice is in it, but justice is found at the cross, which makes forgiveness legally and morally right.*

Jesus took the eternal consequences of sin upon Himself. God "made Him who knew no sin to be sin on our behalf, that we might become the righteousness of God in Him". (2 Corinthians 5:21) We, however, often suffer the temporary consequences of other people's sins. That is simply a harsh reality of life all of us have to face."

- Neil T. Anderson,

The Bondage Breaker [7]

Christ left no room for bitterness when He died on the cross to save us from our sins. Big or small. It's all the same to God, but as humans we give our sins a scale rating and make the smaller ones seem like a lesser evil compared to the ultimate betrayal of our marriage vows. Bitterness will seep into every area of your life, if not forgiven. I've witnessed people divorced for over 30 years still holding grudges against each other due to hearts not allowing forgiveness, friendships ended because of bitter roots, and marriages on the edge of collapse because it's just "too hard" to face the pain and trudge through the emotions. **Bitterness is satan's deceit that robs us of joy.**

Another way the devil uses bitterness is by empowering those who have been hurt to become historic with their spouse. By that I mean in the middle of an argument you yell out in frustration and hurt, "I feel this way because YOU did this to me. It's your fault I'm having a bad day. I did this because you did it first!" Bitterness will show up if forgiveness is not spoken. Like that nasty weed that will keep coming back if not cut at the root, bitterness will continue to resurface if not handled.

We need to remember that we are **all** capable of sinful actions and we all need grace given to us as well. "For **all** have sinned and fall short of the glory of God." Romans 3:23

Betrayal is the HEAT; bitterness becomes one of the revolving consequences that produces bad fruit and pulls us away from Christ. (Refer to the Three Trees Diagram)

Questions for Discussion and Reflection:

- In what ways have revolving consequences pulled you away from God?

Leader Sharing: (example of one leaders sharing - insert your own or use as a guide to discussion)

Common revolving consequences are: anger, resentment, shame, disappointment from unmet expectations, isolation, escapism and fear. There were days when I felt the bitterness of betrayal feeling so unfair. Because of Tim's sinful desires, he invited danger into our marriage and home. He took the risk of following his addiction; in return, I became the one to suffer the injury.

- What bitterness do you have in your life that needs to be brought to the foot of the cross?

Leader Sharing: Growing hatred towards co-workers that live a lifestyle not approved by your own standards or that trigger pain in your life. Hatred or resentment towards family members or friends for not protecting your heart or keeping secrets that have now caused such extreme trauma. A situation not related to you that you know of that shares in similar emotions you're experiencing. A childhood memory that's been brought to the surface.

What joy has satan robbed you of?

Leader Sharing: (Common answers from previous groups.)

freedom, image, dreams, hope in commitment, financial security, the security a complete family brings to children, job environment, emotional security/consistency, intimacy, the joy of growing old together, relationship with children, fear of health concerns due to betrayal - possible STD, fear of continued addiction battles.

- How has releasing your bitterness to the cross set you free and how did God redeem you through that process of forgiveness?

Testimony from a woman who attended our small group:

"I wanted to tell you that at our last meeting, I think God gave me this picture in my mind of a garden. A beautiful garden representing my marriage. And a weed popped up in the garden, which is bitterness. Like you said, in the beginning of betrayal, bitterness will almost be automatic, but it's what we do with it. Sometimes I choose to sit in front of this weed and tell myself the whole garden is ruined. I don't enjoy the rest of the flowers, or the fruits growing. This weed was put there by the enemy, but it won't grow unless we water it and tend to it (i.e. nurse it). If I do pay too much attention to it, water it, nurse it, it will grow quickly. It will take over my entire garden. And if I sit in front of this weed all the time and ignore the rest of the garden, the beautiful flowers will eventually die too. The weed also needs sun to survive, so the way I kill it off is to put it in the shadow of the cross. In the darkness, without water, it won't survive…and my garden will flourish once again. There may be other weeds that pop up every now and again, but I will

still be able to enjoy my garden. I'm learning how to reject the lies the enemy tells, and to choose not to focus on the bitterness, but instead on the good works God is doing in my marriage."

What Does the Bible Say?

- **Psalm 71:20,** "Though You have made me see troubles, many and bitter, You will restore my life again; from the depths of the earth You will bring me up."

Leader Reading and Emphasis: Nelson's Bible Commentary says: Depths of the earth is a metaphor for the psalmist's despondency (40:2); he feels as though he has already dropped headlong into a pit. [8]

- **Ephesians 4:31,** "Get rid of all bitterness, rage and anger, brawling and slander, along with every form of malice."

- **James 3:14-15,** "But if you harbor bitter envy and selfish ambition in your hearts, do not boast about it or deny the truth. Such "wisdom" does not come down from Heaven but is earthly, unspiritual, of the devil."

- **Hebrews 12:15,** "See to it that no one misses the grace of God and that no bitter root grows up to cause trouble and defile many."

- **Romans 12:17-21,** "Do not repay anyone evil for evil. Be careful to do what is right in the eyes of everybody. If it is possible, as far as it depends on you, live at peace with everyone. Do not take revenge, my friends, but leave room for God's wrath, for it is written: "It is mine to avenge; I will repay," says the Lord. On the contrary: "If your enemy is hungry, feed him; if he is thirsty, give him something to drink. In doing this, you will heap burning coals soon his head."

- **Proverbs 14:10,** " Each heart knows its own bitterness, and no one can share its joy."

Leader Reading and Emphasis: Nelson's Bible Commentary says: Only when it is too late does the deluded person discover that he is on the crowded highway to death. The implication is not that he was tricked, but that he relied too heavily on his own "wisdom" rather than turning in humility to God. [9]

Suggested Reflection for the Week: A suggestion this week between class is to journal and note the areas of bitterness you find yourself facing. Bitterness towards your spouse, your family who doesn't understand the situation, friends who aren't supporting well in the moment, etc. What bitterness do you need to call out and face in this moment? The first step to dealing with the bitterness, is identifying it! Use the Reclaimed Blessing Journal or grab a journal of your own.

Shame *(Satan's Bondage of Silence - Hell's duct tape. Place a roll of duct tape on table as visual.)*

We have to consciously make a <u>decision</u> to not let the shame creep over our wounds and make scars of <u>regret</u> or it will separate us from Jesus, isolating us from His plan. At times, it may feel like there is a sign on your back that says: "My spouse betrayed our wedding vows", as shame is like an article of clothing that covers you with embarrassment, guilt, and seems to overwhelm your emotions.

Shame is satan's way of silencing you. It tells us we're not good enough for Jesus or others. Shame caused by betrayal can be paralyzing; it can strip you of every positive thought, memory and celebration you shared with your spouse. Secrecy, silence and self-judgement creates intense disappointment and makes us feel unworthy. There were days where I (Stephanie) caught myself glancing at photographs of our family from pre-confession questioning whether a peek at a pornographic image happened on that trip or in this place of our home. I'd think to myself, "I wonder if something happened when we were here or there? When he came home from this business trip, were the gifts given because of guilt for actions that took place earlier?" As I reviewed our memories, feelings of shame for not protecting my husband at certain vacation spots would overwhelm me. Or opposite, I'd become curious and question the timeline of the addiction and piece together conversations at that moment.

A 2014 article posted on the website, WIRED, written by Christian Jarrett, said this about brain research which is trying to prove that shame / humiliation is the most intense human emotion:

> "Otten and Jonas (a pair of psychologists) said, that shame & humiliation, more than the other emotions they studied, leads to a mobilization of more processing power and a greater consumption of mental resources. This supports the idea that humiliation is a particularly intense and demanding negative emotional experience that has far-reaching consequences for individuals and groups alike. The brain seems to be doing more when you're feeling humiliated, but we don't really know what. One possibility, which in fairness they acknowledge, is that humiliation requires more mental processing, not because it's so intense, but because it's a complex social emotion that involves monitoring loss of social status." [10]

It's no wonder we're so wiped when trying to navigate the emotions and burdens of betrayal, and working through the shame and humiliation it has caused us. We need to be aware that Satan is using this shame and humiliation to render us useless in the moment, and to pull us away from the only thing that can provide the healing we require - Jesus.

There should be no shame in coming before our Savior in these moments, even as raw and ugly as we may feel. God does not judge us for simply feeling. God walks by our side as we work through the emotions of the pain caused against us. Don't let Satan take that experience from you.

Questions for Discussion and Reflection:

- How has shame robbed your heart? How have you been silenced? Who do you blame for the shame in your life? Remember, God created our nervous system, which includes our emotions, so He knows what we're feeling and experiencing in our shame and pain.

Leader Sharing: Not feeling like you're good enough so why even try or speak up since your opinion seems to not matter to others. Fear of anything new has you stuck. Fear of trusting again in friendships or even with family because you feel they'll judge you for what happened in your marriage.

- In what ways have you been able to bring your guilt for your shame to the cross? Being able to recognize cross roads (guilt & shame) and building Godly character out of it is a huge accomplishment. Jesus wants to show up in our shame.

- Has shame changed your lifestyle and your perspective of yourself?

Leader Sharing: Some common responses for women across the board are they present themselves differently. If your husband struggles with lust of the eyes, some women have been more cautious in what or how they wear clothing. Regardless if the marriage was restored as one, many say they're friendships changed because the blinders have been removed and you see the lack of protection, values or morals implemented in others lives which become triggers in yours. The most common with every single broken women who has walked betrayal has been a lack of confidence for a short amount of time or for years after. Shame presents itself in many different ways but this by far has been the most challenging to silence.

- How do you communicate shame? Silent treatment, cold shoulder, retaliation through negative actions, isolation?

Leader Sharing: Brene Brown, TEDx speaker and counselor says, "Vulnerability is not a weakness; it is the most accurate measurement of courage." The link to her TED talk "Listening to Shame" can be found in your weekly email sent earlier. She writes a few books and not all are rooted from a Biblical, Jesus following stance. I only encouraged you to watch the talk simply because of the connection between shame and the weight it carries. [11]

What Does the Bible Say?

- **Isaiah 50:7**, "Because the Sovereign Lord helps me, I will not be disgraced. Therefore I have set my face like flint, (a hard gray rock) and I know I will not be put to shame."

- **Isaiah 61:7**, "Instead of their shame my people will receive a double portion, and instead of disgrace they will rejoice in their inheritance; and so they will inherit a double portion in their land, and everlasting joy will be theirs."

- **1 John 1:9**, "If we confess our sins, he is faithful and just and will forgive us our sins and purify us from all unrighteousness."

- **Genesis 3:10**, "He (Adam) answered, "I heard you in the garden, and I was afraid because I was naked; so I hid."

- **Psalm 34:4-5,** "I sought the Lord, and he answered me; he delivered me from all my fears. Those who look to him are radiant; their faces are never covered in shame."

- **Romans 10:11**, "As the Scriptures says, Anyone who trusts in him will never be put to shame."

- **Isaiah 29:22**, "Therefore this is what the Lord, who redeemed Abraham, says to the house of Jacob: "No longer will Jacob be ashamed; no longer will their faces grow pale."

Grief

"Jesus wept." (John 11:35) In that action alone, God gave us permission to grieve over what **WE** love. This is an important step to take in our journey to healing. **Tears are okay**; it's healthy to let it out rather than bottle everything up inside. Grieve over what was lost and stolen from your relationship. Grieve over the sacred being ripped out of your marriage. Use the emotions to positively propel you forward instead of what some so often do, and stay stuck in the muck. God does allow us to grieve, but, He wants us to find JOY!

That first night, I was told, "Grieve over the death of your marriage. Grieve over the loss of what was, what could have been, and what may be. Your marriage will never look the same and for that you need to grieve for what you lost." Don't think for a minute that you don't have permission or you're on a timeline of grieving. This process looks different for each person and is a vital step to healing and restoration.

Seven Stages of Grief:

1. Shock and Denial
2. Pain and Guilt, Disappointment
3. Anger
4. Bargaining
5. Depression & Sorrow
6. Testing & Reconstruction
7. Acceptance

Leader Sharing: (Fill in the blanks; add in your own personal experiences. Listed are what Stephanie experienced.)

1. Shock & Denial (lack of appetite - didn't eat for 10 days, numbness, tears, no sleep)
2. Pain & Guilt, Disappointment (letter to Tim the day after which was read to him in the Pastors office, resulted in tears, journaling emotions)
3. Anger(Target shopping trip with turtle neck & sweats charging through the store to replace the purging. No one had the right to see any of my skin - I hadn't combed my hair, no bra, probably didn't brush my teeth. My Mom, who was pushing the kids in the shopping cart, walked about ten feet behind me as she was embarrassed by what was happening.)
4. Bargaining (purging - I threw out much of what represented Tim's pornography addiction. Underwear, towels, movies, etc.)
5. Depression & Sorrow (went on anti-depressants for 6 weeks, deep sadness, hard to get out of the funk.)

6. Testing & Reconstruction (asked lots of questions, painted our bedroom, organized many things in the home including our social lives, watched many marriage podcasts, read books and attempted to trust again. This was a stage I parked at for a long time.)
7. Acceptance (forgiveness; sometimes multiple times a day.)

Some days, or even months later, I felt like I made great progress through my grief, but then came triggers, resulting in me landing back to stage one in this revolving process.

Hurt & Anger are HEALTHY emotions. They reveal that you're human. Gary Chapman writes this in the book Desperate Marriages about choosing a response to hurt and anger.

"Hurt and anger are two of the most common emotions upon learning of a spouse's unfaithfulness. These are deep and powerful emotions. In anger, you could pull the trigger and kill the guilty party, or you can turn and walk out the door and never return. One alternative leads to death, the other divorce, but neither deals with the issues that gave rise to the unfaithfulness. And both create another whole set of problems with which you must now deal. Hurt and anger are healthy emotions.

Initially, crying, weeping, and sobbing are healthy response to the emotions of hurt and anger. However, the body is limited in how long it can sustain such agony; thus, sessions of weeping must be interspersed with periods of calm. Verbally expressing your hurt and anger to the unfaithful spouse is a healthy way of processing anger.

It is better if you can express your anger with "I" statements rather than "you" statements, which can sound accusing and provoke a defensive or aggressive response. Any recovery requires that your spouse hear and understand the depth of your hurt and anger.

Verbalizing the hurt and anger to another person is a healthy way of working through the anger to a positive resolution." [12]

Did you know that "DO NOT FEAR" is the most common command in the Bible? [13] As you grieve, consider your destination. Jesus teaches that we will be delivered from evil in all its forms. Don't skip this critical process and stage in your healing journey, but also, don't loose sight of the end matter. (Ecclesiastes 7:8)

Questions for Discussion and Reflection:
- Did you find it hard to grieve, with bitterness lurking around the corner, or did God give you the grace to journey through this step with compassion?

- What negative fruits have birthed out of the grief and betrayal in your marriage? Are you able to recognize the bad fruits, and if so, what are you doing to change them?

- How can we grieve for others without showing guilt (we can show guilt through body language and conversations) for their sins?

Leader Sharing: Some body language that suggests no guilt is showing no judgement, no finger pointing across the soccer field at a kids' team sport, listening rather than forcing opinions, being Jesus to the hurting or guilty verses the cold shoulder or evil eyes. When you see someone in the grocery isle that has caused you to become bitter, rather than turning around and darting before they see you, you keep going about your shopping and not run the other direction. Accepting that we ourselves have caused other people to hurt, should make accepting others who have caused you pain a little easier.

There is a great article that talks about how grief affects our body by Alan D. Wolfelt titled, *"Healing Your Grieving Body: Physical Practices for Mourners."* [14] Whether it's a physical loss or emotional loss, your body will respond in ways you didn't think possible. Many women share they struggle with respiratory related illnesses when going through separation or divorce. Personally, Stephanie has experienced the art of clenching her teeth due to loss and stress. Three days after Tim's confession her body went into shock and she had a day of heavy bleeding even though she had just had her monthly cycle. The embarrassing kind that goes through your pants and you feel like you're back in your junior high days of checking your backside. If you find yourself struggling with a physical illness or hangup, ask yourself if this could potentially be grief related.

What Does the Bible Say?

- **Isaiah 49:13,** "Shout for joy, O heavens; rejoice, O earth; burst into song, O mountains! For the Lord comforts His people and will have compassion on His afflicted ones."

- **Isaiah 43:2,** "When you pass through waters, I will be with you; and when you pass through the rivers, they will not sweep over you. When you walk through the fire, you will not be burned; the flames will not set you ablaze."

- **Matthew 5:4,** "Blessed are those who mourn, for they will be comforted."

- **1 Peter 5:7**, "Cast all your anxiety on Him because He cares for you."

- **Revelation 21:4,** "He will wipe every tear from their eyes. There will be no more death or mourning or crying or pain, for the old order of things has passed away."

Weariness

The moment you stop trying to fix things yourself and <u>acknowledge</u> your need for Him is the moment He shows up to give you <u>strength</u>.

Exhaustion can make us do very funny things, or even stupid things too! I once put a gallon of milk in the cereal cupboard and cereal in the fridge. I was deprived of sleep from spending nearly 4 weeks on the couch with two kids; I was pouring into them so that the situation didn't overwhelm them. I was slowly starting to eat and drink again, attempting a light work schedule and spending many late nights in deep, lengthy renewing conversations with my husband and Jesus. Exhaustion overcame me and depression was lurking around the corner.

In our fast-paced life of jobs, family, relationships, and the household chore list, we find ourselves exhausted at the end of a day, before we even add on the emotional despair that accompanies a broken marriage. It is easy to think that a quick prayer before falling asleep will remedy this exhaustion, but God wants more of us in those weak moments. God will give us the energy to push forward when we allow Him to fuel up our hearts and minds. Making it a habit to start the day and end the day with God, as well as walking with him throughout the day, is just as vital to survival as water. Frankly, it's more vital! Even if you have no strength to get out of bed, find the words to utter a simple plea to the One who is ready to fill you with living sustaining words.

God's <u>grace</u> really is enough to carry <u>you</u> when you feel like <u>you</u> can't walk anymore.

Questions for Discussion and Reflection:

- Do you carve out time each day to spend with God?

Leader Sharing: Daily reading through the Bible (SOAP handout), short devotions, mommy books, self-help, and encouraging Christ-filled blogs. She Reads Truth/He Reads Truth app online devotionals paired with the free LOGOS Bible software to have a deeper, better understanding of the Word. The First 5 by Proverbs 31 Ministries app gives you daily readings with optional reading plans.

Hand out Spiritual inventory, a guide to see where your own heart is. To be done privately; not during group.

- What are some of the "good fruit" that you have been able to notice from your situation? Do you find it hard to produce good fruit when you feel depleted and worn out?

Leader Sharing: some examples would be feeling less judgmental, filled with more grace, more compassionate, head/heart more in tune with God.

- Are you able to recognize your fatigue, and humble yourself enough to ask for help?

Leader Sharing: Sometimes you have to accept that a happy family is more important than a clean, perfect house. Take-out is better than stressing over a 5 course, balanced meal IF it will allow you to have more time in the Word and get back in balance. Check your margins. Ask for accountability to keep your routine, structure, grace and forgiveness.

Remember, through all of your journey towards healing and restoration, that you are in charge of you only. You can influence and example but have no power to change other people as it's their choice to change on their own. Keep your focus vertical (God) before you attempt to reach out horizontally (others).

- What are your essentials to a weary day? Do you rely on your faith to get you through or does your faith need some "working out" so the exhaustion doesn't take over?

Leader Sharing: Stephanie often talks about the 3 essentials: put a bra on, brush the fur off your teeth and slap some deodorant on. These became the least amount of routine for the first few weeks. Sadly, there were days when the fur grew longer and the "ladies" swayed freely because I simply didn't have the strength to do the basics. Turning on some worship music, inviting my go-to's into the weary situation, even allowing Tim into the bad day, was something I had to accept as okay. Open up the blinds, take a shower, go for walk and experience the fresh air.

What Does the Bible Say?

- **Matthew 11:28,** "Come to Me, all who are weary burdened, and I will give you rest."

- **Psalm 62:1-2,** "My soul finds rest in God alone; my salvation does from Him. He alone is my rock and salvation; He is my fortress, I will never be shaken."

- **Romans 12:11,** "Never be lacking in zeal, but keep your spiritual fervor, serving the Lord."

- **Hebrews 12:3,** "Consider Him who endured such opposition from sinful men, so that you will not grow weary and lose heart."

- **Galatians 6:9,** "Let us not become weary in doing good, for at the proper time we will reap a harvest if we do not give up."

- **Isaiah 40:31**, "But those who hope in the Lord will renew their strength. They will soar on wings like eagles; they will run and not grow weary, they will walk and not be faint."

- **Nehemiah 9:20,** "You gave your good Spirit to instruct them. You did not withhold your manna from their mouths, and you gave them water for their thirst."

Leader Reading and Emphasis: Matthew Henry's Concise Commentary says this: Behold this sweet promise, A God ready to pardon! Instead of keeping away from God under a sense of unworthiness, let us come boldly to the throne of grace, that we may obtain mercy, and find grace to help in time of need. He is a God ready to pardon. [15]

Image

*When we don't realize who we are in Christ, **our faith will be crippled.** If you don't feel worthy to exercise your authority in Christ, then you won't be doing it in the fullness of faith and will lack assurance. Satan works diligently to program people's minds to feel unworthy and unable to walk in power of God here on earth. This is one of the most popular strongholds in existence today in the body of Christ! The truth is that we, by our own power and effort, are unworthy, but it is the Blood of Christ that makes us worthy. And if we say we are unworthy when the Blood says we are, then we are denying the work that Christ did for us on the cross!*

- Online article [16]

It is critical to know <u>who you are</u> in Christ as you offer yourself to your marriage. Husband and wife need to have <u>individual</u> relationships with their risen Savior and <u>then together</u>, share a Christ-like union in their vows. If not, you will find yourself lost, drained, and depleted of everything you are. Being able to stand strong in your presentation and depiction of God is an important aspect of the shared relationship. Your <u>identity</u> is NOT found in the sins of the past or web of <u>consequences</u> from the mistakes in your marriage. Your identity is <u>found</u> in the risen <u>Savior</u>!

The majority of women walking through betrayal have expressed how devastated their self-image is after picking up the shattered pieces of their marriage. This has been the most challenging sin consequence resulting from Tim's confession. Here's how mislead my ideas of image were right after Tim's confession....

The first Sunday we went to church together after Tim had moved back home, I remember standing next to this guy with his hands raised singing praises to God during worship. "Who is this person? What is my role now?" When we got home, I collapsed in bed and sobbed in fear of who I was not, fear of who I was becoming and confusion about who this new person was, I was still married to was now. God had taken this broken, beat up life of my husband's and made him new. I was left to watch and wonder in attempts to figure out where I fit into this new renewed life. It took me a long time and counsel to figure out who I was in Christ again.

A few months post confession, Tim was given a revelation though a mentor that really explained all my new fears. His selfish addictions stripped me of who I was over the years, and in doing so killed the very person he married, depleting so much of what I worked for. The devil knew this would become my weak spot and I have to fight against the urge to believe in his lies daily. This goes beyond the title of wife, mom, or co-worker. There are days where it takes me five outfits to finally decide on the one okay outfit to leave the house. My eyes for years saw a worthless, unqualified and not-good enough person to those I offered relationship to.

God continues to speak truth to me and squashes out the lies I believed about myself. Being in God's Word has been the biggest defense against the sin consequence of my mind.

Questions for Discussion and Reflection:

- How do you think people view you? (Do people see you as a trustworthy, honest person?) If you had to write on a note card attributes about yourself, what would they be? Would they look different if you had your spouse write them or a close friend?

Leader sharing: (insert your own personal stories or share Stephanie's)

Talk about how image was, and still can be, the biggest sin consequence the confession brought into our lives. (From Stephanie: The air brushed images my husband viewed ripped my confidence away as a wife and woman in society. I can never compare to that status. The pornography addiction was far more destructive then the reality of Tim having multiple affairs. The things I started to believe about myself were devastating to how I viewed myself as a person, woman, wife and mother. I had more work post-confession in this area, and still do, then almost all other areas.

LET'S PRACTICE!

Leader Sharing: Hand out the Reclaimed Lies postcards and take a few minutes to invite the group to write down their facts & fantasies, their truths and lies. As the women are writing these out, expect some to be emotional as they put words to the lies Satan has been telling them since their own personal discovery or confession. Pray over the women as they do this. You can also read out loud from the "Who I Am In Christ" handout and then end in a word of prayer committing these lies and truths to God. Suggest that the women take these postcards home and pray privately, with or without their spouse, then once done rip or burn them up. Some women have written the lies on rocks then thrown them into the nearest river or body of water allowing the lies to sink to the bottom of the ocean. If you feel the women are comfortable sharing their lies with everyone in the group you may do so at this time or continue to the next discussion question. Hand out postcard of "Who I Am In Christ" This is a postcard that states who you are in Christ with scripture verses to back up the truth.

- Where or what do you find your identity rooted in? (Do you define yourself from your past? Is your identity in your looks? Do you seek approval from family first?)

- What evidence is there that Christ is working in your life?

- Do your words match your actions? Is your faith visible to those around you?

What Does the Bible Say?

- **2 Corinthians 5:17,** "Therefore, if anyone is in Christ, he is a new creation; the old has gone, the new has come!"

- **Romans 8:1,** "Therefore, there is now no condemnation for those who are in Christ Jesus."

- **1 Peter 2:9,** "But you are a chosen people, a royal priesthood, a holy nation, a people belonging to God, that you may declare the praises of Him who called you out of darkness into his wonderful light."

- **John 15:5,** "I am the vine; you are the branches. If a man remains in me and I in him, he will bear much fruit; apart from me you can do nothing."

- **Philippians 3:20,** "But our citizenship is in heaven. And we eagerly await a Savior from there, the Lord Jesus Christ."

- **2 Timothy 1:7,** "For God did not give us a spirit of timidity, but a spirit of power, of love and of self-discipline."

- **Colossians 1:13-14,** "For he has rescued us from the dominion of darkness and brought us into the kingdom of the Son he loves, in whom we have redemption, the forgiveness of sins."

"God hath given you one face, and you make yourself another."
-William Shakespeare, Hamlet

Forgiveness - Hand out Forgiveness bookmark

"When a deep injury is done to us, we never heal until we forgive."
- Nelson Mandela

God didn't wait to be crucified until we fully understood the impact His death would have on us. He <u>died</u>. He <u>forgave</u>. He <u>gave</u> us life. Luke 23:34 says, "Father forgive them, for they do not know what they are doing." We need to respond in the same way; challenging ourselves to look past the scars and sometimes bloody mess, to offer forgiveness to those who have hurt us the worst because God did the same for you and for me. We <u>need</u> to forgive as we have been forgiven.

Inter-human evils, those done against and to other people, are some of the hardest situations to overcome. Such evils can be the hardest to forgive when done between husbands and wives, children and parents, co-workers and friends. The pain of betrayal makes for a very crucible experience. Webster Dictionary defines crucible as; "a severe test; a place or situation in which concentrated forces interact to cause or influence change or development." Walking through such a test will undoubtedly change who you are. The behaviors and choices that got you to this point, whether they were your choices made or not, should influence how your life will look like in the future. You won't forget the situation that brought such pain, but you **do not** need to endlessly <u>revisit</u> what happened. Forgiveness is the puzzle piece that will begin that process.

*"**We need to forgive others so Satan cannot take advantage of us.** We are commanded to get rid of all bitterness in our lives. Forgiving yourself is accepting the truth that God has already forgiven you in Christ. Forgiveness is not forgetting. **Once you choose to forgive someone, then Christ can come and begin to heal you of your hurts.** But the healing cannot begin until you first forgive. Forgiveness is mainly a matter of obedience to God. God wants you to be free; there is no other way. Don't wait until you feel like forgiving, You will never get there. Make the hard choice to forgive even if you don't feel like it. **Once you choose to forgive, Satan will have lost his power over you in that area, and God's healing touch will be free to move.**"*

Neil T. Anderson
The Bondage Breaker [17]

Over time, there are purposeful intentions that come out of the fire of evil. God is in this with us and up to something good.

What is forgiveness?

- Forgiveness is not letting the betrayer off the hook. We can, and should, still hold each other accountable for our actions, or lack of actions, in love as Christ did for us.

- Forgiveness is returning to God the right to take care of justice. It's not our job to punish people for their sins.

Leader Insight: Understand forgiveness as a trade instead of holding a person responsible to fix and make things right or pay for their wrong. You are now holding onto Jesus to fix and make things right then redeem the wrong. In other words, by extending forgiveness to someone, you are allowing God to be judge rather than deciding a sentence for the sin yourself.

- Forgiveness does not mean we have to revert to being the victim. Forgiveness is an attitude.

- Forgiveness is not the same as reconciling. We can forgive someone even if we never can get along with him again. Forgiveness benefits the one offering it more than the one receiving it.

- If they don't repent, we still have to forgive. Even if they never ask, we need to forgive. We should memorize and repeat over and over: Forgiveness is about **our** attitude, not their action.

- Living with unforgiveness is like drinking the poison thinking the other person is going to die.

"A betrayer's humble repentance in word and deed will pave the way for the betrayed to again risk opening his or her heart and offering the sweet fruit of forgiveness that can lead to restoration and renewed joy."
- Tim Jackson

Questions for Discussion and Reflection:
- Are there areas in your life where forgiveness is needed?

Leader sharing: Example of couple writing every sexual sin on a piece of paper then praying for each sin as they black them out. This couple first spent the weekend remembering and writing down every sexual sin the husband could remember from his lifetime. Once he was confident he had all his sins on paper, the wife then took the paper and begin forgiving each sin, crossing off each sin with black marker once she forgave her husband. Forgiveness looks different to different people. What works for one person/couple most likely won't work for another. Don't compared forgiveness stories or feel you need it to look a certain way.

- What is your attitude towards God when given the choice to forgive the one who hurt you? Do you feel like you rise above it and allow the good consequence to shine or find justice in the bitterness having sarcasm, anger and stewing rage be the fruit you produce? Do you feel challenged when God tells you to forgive?

What Does the Bible Say?

- **Ephesians 4:31-32,** "Get rid of all bitterness, rage and anger, brawling and slander, along with every form of malice. Be kind and compassionate to one another, forgiving each other, just as in Christ God forgave you."

- **Luke 6:37,** "Do not judge, and you will not be judged. Do not condemn, and you will not be condemned. Forgive, and you will be forgiven."

- **Mark 11:25,** "And when you stand praying, if you hold anything against anyone, forgive him, so that your Father in heaven may forgive you your sins."

- **Matthew 6:15,** "But if you do not forgive men their sins, your Father will not forgive your sins."

- **James 5:16,** "Therefore confess your sins to each other and pray for each other so that you may be healed. The prayer of a righteous man is powerful and effective."

- **Acts 2:38,** "Peter replied, "Repent and be baptized, every one of you, in the name of Jesus Christ for the forgiveness of your sins. And you will receive the gift of the Holy Spirit."

- **Gen. 50:17-21,** "This is what you are to say to Joseph: I ask you to forgive your brothers the sins and the wrongs they committed in treating you so badly.' Now please forgive the sins of the servants of the God of your father." When their message came to him, Joseph wept. His brothers then came and threw themselves down before him. "We are your slaves," they said. But Joseph said to them, "Don't be afraid. Am I in the place of God? You intended to harm me, but God intended it for good to accomplish what is now being done, the saving of many lives. So then, don't be afraid. I will provide for you and your children." And he reassured them and spoke kindly to them."

- **Numbers 14:20,** "The Lord replied, "I have forgiven them, as you asked."

- **Micah 7:18, "**Who is a God like you, who pardons sin and forgives the transgression of the remnant of his inheritance? You do not stay angry forever but delight to show mercy."

There is no reason to forgive unless you believe in something bigger than yourself.

"To be a Christian means to forgive the inexcusable because
Christ has forgiven the inexcusable in us."
- C.S.Lewis

Hope

Hand out hand soap (No need to break the bank on soap. Bath and Body Works if on sale or Dial $1 per bottle are Stephanie's choices from past groups.) - everyday reminder that OUR sins, OUR filth is washed away. There is hope found in starting fresh, new and clean, every morning. Every time you are feeling overwhelmed with the weight of betrayal and the fallout that follows, ask God to wash your mind and heart free of the sins residue. Remember, the focus is on our hearts as we seek healing. We can't change those around us but we have the opportunity to build our own character through our journey.

"Come now, let us reason together, says the Lord; though your sins are like scarlet, they shall be as white as snow; though they are red like crimson, they shall become like wool." Isaiah 1:18

"The way we go after opportunities reveals what we're made of.
The dew of blessing; the critical part of a Christian's gaze recognizing the blessings and goodness in a situation that also function to reveal the human heart."
- David Powlison

I wish hope was found as easily as dust bunnies quickly cluster together. Somedays it may feel like you need to tear down the walls of Jericho in order to see just a glimmer of hope shine through to your soul and other days it may shine through so brightly, like a clear sunny afternoon. It's in the moments where the sun is shining through and you sense progress and see hope, that you also see the dirt and smudges from the stresses of life too. Hope is not an emotion; it's an <u>action</u>. We have to actively work on seeing the <u>best</u> in our situations and seeing God in the little moments weaving everything together for His <u>purpose</u> and His plan. Emotions can derail us from the progress much like the dirt and smudges on the windows allowing our vision to be clouded and blurred. God wants us to not see the stains, but instead the rays of hope shining through.

The fragrance of Christ appears in the context of having been sinned against, and is seen as mercy, forgiveness, courage, endurance, and the ability to **persevere in hope**.

Questions for Discussion and Reflection:
* What has hope looked like to you? Was it a person, a book, a rainbow, or something physical like a brush of a shoulder that indicated the road was turning upwards?

Leader Sharing: When my husband (Tim) and I (Stephanie) were in the process of adopting our daughter Myriam, we found ourselves shy $800 from having the adoption completely funded. At that point, we had exhausted our options with multiple garage sales, bake sales and support letters. One Sunday, after just coming home from church, our door bell rang to which I answered and found no one standing near the front door. As I went to close the door I looked down to find a white envelope placed on our front steps. When I looked inside, I found $800 cash with no note, no name. Just the exact amount of cash we needed to fund our adoption. Immediately after I opened the envelope and called for Tim, a rainbow colored hot air balloon flew right over our house, nearly clipping the tops of the trees. It was a modern day Noah's Ark; a rainbow and white dove example of hope delivered directly to our front porch.

There was also hope found through love notes in my bathroom drawer. Tim had begun the 40 Day Challenge, presented in The Love Dare, based off of the movie Fireproof. I hated this at first; found it repulsive honestly. God knew I needed to be pursued by Tim to see that the romance and intimacy could be brought back to life again.

- Has it been hard to see through the smudges on the window? What do you do when you lose focus?

Leader Sharing: Examples from other women: crank up the music, worship, go for a run, PRAY & get in the WORD, communicate with my spouse so he can surround me and support me in prayer as well. Call my accountability partners.

It's okay to have a healthy fear of starting over again.

"To love means loving the unlovable. To forgive means pardoning the unpardonable. Faith means believing the unbelievable. Hope means hoping when everything seems hopeless."
- G.K. Chesterton

What Does the Bible Say?

- **Job 5:16,** "So the poor have hope, and injustice shuts its mouth."

- **Psalm 9:18,** "But God will never forget the needy; the hope of the afflicted will never perish."

- **Psalm 33:22,** "May your unfailing love be with us, Lord, even as we put our hope in You."

- **Jeremiah 17:7,** "But blessed is the one who trusts in the Lord, whose confidence is in Him."

- **Joel 3:16,** "The Lord will roar from Zion and thunder from Jerusalem; the earth and the heavens will tremble. But the Lord will be a refuge for His people, a stronghold for the people of Israel."

- **Lamentations 3:25-26,** "The Lord is good to those whose hope is in Him, to the one who seeks Him; it is good to wait quietly for the salvation of the Lord."

- **Jeremiah 29:11,** "For I know the plans I have for you," declares the Lord, "plans to prosper you and not to harm you, plans to give you hope and a future."

Hope is God taking the impossible and giving you the strength to believe in the possible. I hope for my children to find Godly men and women to marry someday as they embark on this adult relationship stuff. I hope for Christ to come and save me from more pain before I experience it.

Hope is real. Hope is within our reach and God wants us to hope with great excitement in His expectation. It's what gets us to take that first step towards forgiveness, reconciliation, and sometimes that first hug we crave so intensely. Hope is part of a believers DNA and let us not forget it when life is completely out of control. "I wait for the Lord, my soul waits, and in His word I put my hope." **Psalm 130:5**

Further Questions for Discussion and Reflection:

- Is your hope in God? Do you believe He will overcome your pain?

In the dark dreary nights, when the storm is at its most fierce, the lighthouse burns bright so the sailors can find their way home again. In life the same light burns. This light is fueled with love, faith, and hope. And through life's most fierce storms these three burn their brightest so we also can find our way home again.

-Unknown

Additional Bible Verses

- **Psalm 62:5,** "Find rest, O my soul, in God alone; my hope comes from Him."

- **John 16:33,** "I have told you these things, so that in me you may have peace. In this world you will have trouble. But take heart! I have overcome the world."

- **Romans 8:18,** "I consider that our present sufferings are not worth comparing with the glory that will be revealed in us. The creation waits in eager expectation for the sons of God to be revealed."

- **Matthew 19:26,** "Jesus looked at them and said, "with man this is impossible, but with God, all things are possible."

- **Romans 5:3-5,** "Not only so, but we also rejoice in our sufferings, because we know that suffering produces perseverance, character; and character, hope. And hope does not disappoint us, because God has poured out His love into our hearts, by the Holy Spirit, whom He has given us."

Trust

"Can trust be reborn? Yes, if integrity is reborn. Trust dies when integrity dies."
Gary Chapman

Trusting God after a painful betrayal in your marriage is like standing on a cliff near the Grand Canyon as God says, "I've got this. Trust me and I will <u>protect</u> you, guide you, and give you what you need in this desperate time of suffering and anguish." Getting to the point where you can fall; eyes upward and heart in His hands; knowing all you need is to trust and obey, is so much easier said than done but <u>necessary</u> in your process to healing. (Please no cliff jumping. That's not what I'm encouraging!) When all is resolved and we reflect and see that God ultimately had our back, and our life was taken care of, it's easier to trust Him the next time we are faced with difficult circumstances. The same is true for our marriages. Trusting a spouse after betrayal takes a repetitive behavioral pattern of honesty and transparency, allowing the betrayed into choices that prove the betrayer is again worthy of trust.

Life experiences can make it hard to trust others with our hearts. I've been hurt by some of my closest friends and family members. It has made me cautious as to whom I share life with and whom I offer deep friendship to. BUT, God has never wavered and we can always run to Him, even when it is scary. Placing trust and hope in God means allowing Him to take you places you've never been before; to put you in uncomfortable situations which will result in experiencing His love in ways never thought possible. Often that means pausing mid-journey to reflect on the beauty in the pain, and to remind yourself that you can trust in Him as His will is perfected in your situation. And so goes the hymn...

"Trust and obey, for there's no other way
To be happy in Jesus, but to trust and obey.

When we walk with the Lord in the light of His Word,
What a glory He sheds on our way!
While we do His good will, He abides with us still,
And with all who will trust and obey.

Not a shadow can rise, not a cloud in the skies,
But His smile quickly drives it away;
Not a doubt or a fear, not a sigh or a tear,
Can abide while we trust and obey.

Not a burden we bear, not a sorrow we share,

But our toil He doth richly repay;

Not a grief or a loss, not a frown or a cross,

But is blessed if we trust and obey.

But we never can prove the delights of His love

Until all on the altar we lay;

For the favor He shows, for the joy He bestows,

Are for them who will trust and obey.

Then in fellowship sweet we will sit at His feet.

Or we'll walk by His side in the way.

What He says we will do, where He sends we will go;

Never fear, only trust and obey. [18]

Questions for Discussion and Reflection:

- Have there been situations in your life that have caused you to not trust others and your spouse completely? (etc. childhood trauma, betrayal within friendships or between co-workers, dysfunctional family dynamics)

Leader Sharing: (Stephanie's comments for her group) Tim and Stephanie have each others passwords for their computers and phones. They have apps on their phones to locate where they are and have permission to ask about their location at all times. They regularly check each others text messages to provide transparency into their conversations with others which allows them both to feel accountable with each other. All these things were done more frequently immediately following Tim's confession as trust was being rebuilt. Stephanie asked many hard questions regarding the sin but in the end, the answers gave her what she needed to trust Tim with her heart again. This was not something that happened overnight.

- Do you give others close to you reasons to trust you and do you allow transparency within your marriage? (etc. Can people trust you with a secret or are you known to have a loose mouth?)

- If God threw you in the lions den, is your faith strong enough to trust in the promise of the Word knowing that God is with you?

What Does the Bible Say?

- **Proverbs 3:5,** "Trust in the Lord with all your heart, and lean not on your own understanding."

- **Jeremiah 17:7,** "But blessed is the man who trusts in the Lord, whose confidence is in Him."

- **Psalm 56:3,** "When I am afraid, I will trust in You."

- **Daniel 6:23,** "The king was overjoyed and gave orders to lift Daniel out of the den. And when Daniel was lifted from the Den, no wound was found on him, because he had trusted in his God."

- **Joshua 1:9,** "Have I not commanded you? Be strong and courageous. Do not be terrified; do not be discouraged. For the Lord your God will be with you wherever you go."

- **Isaiah 41:10,** "So do not fear, for I am with you; do not be dismayed, for I am your God. I will strengthen you and help you; I will uphold you with my righteous right hand."

Education

Understanding the grip the enemy has over our minds and everyday life is crucial to protecting our marriages. "Covenant Eyes," is an internet accountability and filtering program which states these facts about the suffocating addiction of pornography:

75% of pastors do not make themselves accountable to anyone.

37% of pastors said viewing pornography was a "current struggle." [19]

81 million daily average visits to Pornhub, the world's most popular porn website. [20]

$20 billion annually is profited/generated globally from the pornography industry. [21]

1 in 5 mobile searches are for pornography. [22]

Leader Sharing: A few additional facts...
• Men are visually oriented; women are emotional and we verbally process things/life that comes at us.
• Porn: the first look is automatic and purely biological; the second look you have a choice of what to do about it, unless you sought it out in the first place.
• Adam and Eve: God created as one giving them a bond between husband and wife. Only sexual sighting was designed to be for your wife or husband.

Some marriages today have a lack of understanding and never give thought to furthering their marital education. We get our college degree, exchange our "I do's", and then relish in the newlywed state of marriage for a few years, sometimes less. Then life happens, children appear, jobs overwhelm, and we are overtaken by daily routines mixed with household chores and driving kids from sports to school. How is it that we put thousands of dollars into a piece of paper that possibly will gain us a career and most often requires continued education, but we can't seem to prioritize the continuing education required for our marriage? It happens so slowly that we don't see it coming, but married life becomes something of "college roommates" passing in the halls. We loose the ZEST in our relationship.

Leader Insight: (Mention the song Slow Fade by Casting Crowns. Suggestion to attach the link to the music video in the post meeting email. The music video is powerful as you watch a man slowly be groomed by the Enemy and eventually caving to the bait. Shows the progression of sin without proper protection and boundaries in place.) [23]

Part of our continued marriage education should be installing "firewalls" in our daily routines to guard against "viruses" that mess with our thought process, make us stumble and lose our focus on the prize. Kids, ages 6-8, are being exposed for the first time to pornography. A stick of gum is being marketed with sex. Walking through a mall is eye candy to any weak mind that seeks lust before God. We have become numb to what we expose ourselves to and need to take back control within our marriage and home to what is first in our lives; Jesus.

It is imperative to know the "why" behind the confession or discovery. If you don't know what is broken, you don't know what to fix. Once you locate the cause, the catalyst to the confession, then you can install protective measures to guard against further fatal discoveries. This may mean you need to pull back layers, past years possibly back to your childhood, to resolve your why.

Questions for Discussion and Reflection:

- Is there a lack of "continued education" within your marriage? (Do/Did you read books, do devotions, pray together or go on dates to grow your marriage?)

- Are you intimidated by marriage conferences? Why? What would you want to see offered with regard to conferences/aids to marriages?

- Do you fear knowing more about your vows or do you trust God to reveal a deeper knowledge within your marriage commitment to each other? (What's holding you back from committing?)

- What are some ways that you have grown deeper in your marriage?

- What are some other ways we can guard ourselves, educate our marriages, and show others our respect for our spouses when in public?

Suggestions to guarding your home from the pull of lust: Prescreen all movies and TV shows before watching. There are phone apps where you can read more in depth about a movie or TV show before viewing. Apple TV, Netflix or Hulu all have limited commercials. This eliminates many offensive and suggestive commercials. The mailbox may be a stumbling block for your spouse. Magazines, catalogs, and other junk mail often have provocative images on the front pages. Maybe put one person in charge to gather the mail and throw away anything that could become a trigger into an addiction. This also protects the young men in your home from grabbing a publication and hiding it for a later time. Don't just think about the adult men in your home. Their are little eyes being exposed to such images that are almost impossible to erase from the mind. Set up a boundary that certain places are off limits; eating establishments, beaches, vacation spots, bars or quite possibly a group of friends.

Suggested websites to educate and protect:

www.covenanteyes.net

www.integrityrestored.com

www.qustodio.com

www.fightthenewdrug.org

www.netnanny.com

www.IMDb.com

Some men find a telephone pole attractive, so living like a cave man is not an option. It is through healthy boundaries and education as a couple, that can defeat the mind. (Hiding away, locking yourself and family up in a hole will not fix the problem. Sin will find you.)

"For the word of God is living and active. Sharper than any double-edge sword, it penetrates even to dividing soul and spirit, joints and marrow; it judges the thoughts and attitudes of the heart."

Hebrews 4:12

What Does the Bible Say?

- **Proverbs 1:5,** "Let the wise listen and add to their learning, and let the discerning get guidance."

- **Proverbs 9:9,** "Instruct a wise man and he will be wiser still; teach a righteous man and he will add to his learning."

- **Proverbs 18:15,** "The heart of the discerning requires knowledge; the ears of the wise seek it out."

- **Ephesians 1:17,** "I keep asking that the God of our Lord Jesus Christ, the glorious Father, will give you the Spirit of wisdom and revelation, so that you may know Him better."

- **Colossians 1:9,** "For this reason, since the day we heard about you, we have not stopped praying for you and asking God to fill you with the knowledge of His will, through all spiritual wisdom and understanding."

Communication

      Being able to have <u>transparent</u> communication in your relationship and finding new ways to <u>express</u> your love towards each other will not only build trust, but strengthen your vows. Gary Chapman in his book, *The Five Love Languages*, helps us discover what our love languages are and how vital it is to speak each others language in a marriage.

      (**The Five Love Languages:** Physical Touch, Words of Affirmation, Acts of Service, Quality Time, and Gifts)[24]

      Allow your tone of voice, body language, and ability to speak in love, expand your relationship to the next level as you both <u>rediscover</u> your new marriage. Sometimes that means going outside your comfort zone and having to discuss what you're REALLY thinking. This is hard, but trust me, the more honest and vulnerable you can be, generally will inspire the other to open up and meet you with the same vulnerability.

      This may take a pile of humility on your part to sit and listen, but allow God to quiet you or quiet your spouse so you can really hear each others heart. Maybe start out simple by asking how the day was, or dive in and compliment your spouse with one reason why you appreciate them. This may be challenging if you are in a position of separation or divorce. Don't let that stop you. You have little eyes around you that are watching how you respond to this conflict. It's your choice to let the bad fruit spew out or the good fruit shine. (refer to the three tree diagram)

Questions for Discussion and Reflection:

Leader Example: Love Language #6: Strap & Straddle; Put a helmet on! Stephanie has added a 6th language to Gary's list of Love Languages. Her husband has a love for risking his life on a motorcycle and nothing speaks louder than straddling a death trap while Stephanie's grip around his waist tightens. A great reminder that we each speak and receive love differently and you may need to get creative to best meet each others needs within your marriage.

- Do you sometimes feel like you're the only one who understands what is coming out of your mouth?

Leader Sharing: View your communication like an iceberg: Are you only talking about what you see on the surface or have you dove into the deep emotional levels of communication that expose the true heart condition? Some husbands (and kids) quite possibly think you speak a different language; keep it simple and to the point.

4 Common Responses That Can Ruin Relationships: Hand out 4 Response card

1. **Fight:** You attack others when you feel fearful; intimidating the other people; you have unreasonable demands that try to control the situation.

2. **Flight:** You find yourself busy with distractions; sleeping, hyper-activity, always gone doing things, never home, binge on Netflix.

3. **Freeze:** You give-up, blank-out, feel stuck, and hold breath in dread; dissociation, escapism.

4. **Fawn:** You tend to be a people pleaser; constantly walking on egg shells. You rarely show the real you to those around you.

- Which is your most common coping mechanism when feeling fearful, insecure or threatened?

- How is that coping mechanism affecting your marriage or other relationships?

- How has your body language changed the tone of conversation with others, and with your spouse?

Leader Sharing: Make a special "code" for those moments when there are no words. If there are children in the home, create a symbol that can act as a silent "time out" to express that right now is not the time, I need space, or I'm not wanting to talk about this right now. If you're in a social setting, create hand gestures to indicate "You're getting too close, you're getting too loud, you have crossed a line and out of control - we're leaving!"

- When discussing the raw heart issues in your marriage, do you find yourself speaking in humility and love, or anger and bitterness?

What Does the Bible Say?

- **Ephesians 4:29,** "Do not let any unwholesome talk come out of your mouths, but only what is helpful for building others up according to their needs, that it may benefit those who listen."

- **Hebrews 4:12,** "For the word of God is alive and active. Sharper than any doubled-edged sword, it penetrates even to dividing soul and spirit, joints and marrow; it judges the thoughts and attitudes of the heart."

- **James 1:19,** "Everyone should be quick to listen, slow to speak, and slow to become angry."

- **Psalm 19:14,** "May the words of my mouth and the meditation of my heart be pleasing in your sight, O Lord, my Rock and my Redeemer."

- **Proverbs 15:1,** "A gentle answer turns away wrath, but a harsh word stirs up anger."

- **Proverbs 12:18,** "Reckless words pierce like a sword, but the tongue of the wise brings healing."

- **Proverbs 16:24,** "Pleasant words are a honeycomb, sweet to the soul and healing to the bones."

Support

Do you remember playing the childhood game "Telephone"? You sit in a circle and start by whispering in one person's ear a statement and by the time it reaches the other end, the statement is twisted, backwards, and nowhere near the statement first spoken. It can be hilarious to see how fast the story can change and be altered simply because people aren't listening intently or are in a rush and say something backwards. Same goes for when you say something in confidence to a friend or in passing to someone that asks, "How are you doing?" It always amazes me how quickly stories can be changed for the worse if not protected.

I was once told to protect my story as it was mine to share when I felt compelled to share and when I felt safe enough to bring light to my marital situation. For years after Tim and I went through our dark valley, just our immediate family, pastors, and two close friends knew the struggles we were dealing with. I had a few clients who knew, but it was only because of tears, or having to reschedule appointments, that they found out. We knew that in order to fix us we had to protect our journey by keeping silence so outside opinions and games of "telephone" didn't work against our progress. We surrounded our little family with those that would uplift us, pray for us and stand behind us in the trenches. Anything outside of that would have just been noise, and a distraction from the hard work we needed to complete.

Jesus did the same as He performed miracles when walking on this earth. Jesus had His 12 disciples come alongside Him to pray for Him, support Him, and set the story straight when whispers started to spread.

Questions for Discussion and Reflection:

- Are you taking measures to protect YOUR story? (Do you find yourself talking to everyone about all the details of the addiction or affair? Do you believe you are entitled to share with anyone? When you do share, are you speaking with a negative tone? Is that in front of an audience, your kids, family or co-workers? How is your sharing reflecting the Jesus that lives inside of you? Do you radiate Christ?

- Have you been supportive & respectful of your spouse when sharing your story?

Leader Sharing: Do you have accountability couples, brothers or sisters in Christ to hold you to the growth moving forward? What support have you placed in your home to protect your marriage? Many couples who are pursuing restoration have daily, weekly and monthly accountability people that are a phone call away. Some couples make Recovery Plans that clearly lay out consequences if the behavior were to continue. Celebrate Recovery is one fantastic way to both seek mentors in healing. Also, ask your local church for a list of Christian counselors that are trained and experienced for your journey.

What Does the Bible Say?

- **Acts 15:32,** "Judas and Silas, who themselves were prophets, said much to encourage and strengthen the believers."

- **Romans 15:7,** "Accept one another, then, just as Christ accepted you, in order to bring praise to God."

- **Hebrews 10:24,** "And let us consider how we may spur one another on toward love and good deeds."

- **Galatians 6:2,** "Carry each other's burdens, and in this way you will fulfill the law of Christ."

- **Romans 12:11,13,** "Never be lacking in zeal, but keep your spiritual fervor, serving the Lord… Share with the Lord's people who are in need. Practice hospitality."

Restoration: building blocks
Bring building blocks & yard clippers to class. Suggestions for building blocks are to write things needed to reclaim the broken relationship and person. Etc. Jesus, Trust, Intimacy, Joy, Communication, Confidence.

The Vinedresser does not start with the clippers; He starts with the snips.

"Love is an art to be learned and a discipline to be maintained."
- Ed Wheat

"I am the vine; you are the branches. If a man remains in me and I in him, he will bear much fruit; apart from me you can do nothing. My command is this: Love each other as I have loved you. Greater love has no one than this, that he lay down his life for his friends."
John 15:5,12-13

Building a new marriage means you "create the sacred" in the marriage again. You must learn to cherish your spouse and be transparent with each other.

In Biblical times, people grew a hedge of thorns around their gardens and even their houses as a method of protection. Likewise, we need to build a hedge of protection around our marriages. Job 1:10 says, "Have you not put a hedge around him and his household and everything he has? You have blessed the work of his hands, so that his flocks and herds are spread throughout the land."

We must agree to not take any chances with our marriage when trying to protect and restore what was broken. Aspects of the hedge can be found in education, through proper support and counsel, ultimately in cementing your faith in the One who can restore even the ugliest of sins.

Nothing lasting happens overnight. It takes time, God will reward you for the decision to choose restoration, and He will grant you the patience needed as you make mistakes and work together to change. God will not judge and wants us to follow His example when we confess to one another and seek transparency in our relationships. You might not see progress when comparing to the day before, but over time, with God's help, you will see a beautifully restored and renewed marriage.

The restoration and purification of your heart and marriage is one of the prime works of the Holy Spirit. He (God) will shake you loose, set you free and grant you patience for the process. Remember the process gold must go through to get to its pure state. It must endure the fire to burn off the rubbish or it will always just be a dull, shapeless lump. It is in the process of going through the fire that all the not-so-glorious parts are burned off to allow the perfect and beautiful parts to shine brightly.

Leader suggestion: The book *"Making All Things New"* by David Powlison is a suggested book to read that details more ways to restore the sexual scars in your life.

Questions for Discussion and Reflection:

- How has God given you patience to mend and restore what was broken? (Take your spouse out of the equation and answer this for yourself.)

Leader Sharing: Some steps to Restoration: 1. Summarize what you are restoring; ask God to bring all that needs mending to the surface followed by forgiveness. 2. Pray; ask God to comfort you both as you seek restoration and to give you listening ears. 3. Own what is yours. 4. List what you need to make restoration possible. 5. Be firm; but also know you may need to compromise. 6. Boundaries; they need to be tested. Set dates to achieve goals, tasks and needs. 7. Forgiveness. 8. More prayer. 9. Forgiveness. 10. Reevaluate the situation if not working.

- Do you feel you have the tools necessary to remodel your relationship? If not, have you found the courage to speak up and ask for help?

"You don't have the luxury of planning even the next sentence to come out of your mouth. You immediately publish the distempers or radiancies of your soul. You publish by the questions you ask (or don't ask), by how you listen (or don't really want to listen), by the interpretations you offer (or don't even think to offer), by the advice you give (or can't give), by the attitude you take towards people, towards problems and towards people with problems."
-David Powlison

- Locating your current struggles, and identifying what they mean, allows you to see what exactly is at stake and where you are going. Are you able to locate your situation (the heat) and see the difference between truth and lies? The restoration process can only begin when you allow God to start pruning your own heart. (Refer to the Three Trees Diagram)

- What are some ways that you have restored your marriage and God has healed your heart? If the marriage dissolved in a divorce, have you been able to see restoration within other relationships that surrounded your marriage?

Remember a small start can lead to big change!

What Does the Bible Say?

- **Psalm 91 - The Prayer of Protection:** Whoever dwells in the shelter of the Most High will rest in the shadow of the Almighty. I will say of the Lord, "He is my refuge and my fortress, my God, in whom I trust." Surely he will save you from the fowler's snare and from the deadly pestilence. He will cover you with his feathers, and under his wings you will find refuge; his faithfulness will be your shield and rampart. You will not fear the terror of night, nor the arrow that flies by day, nor the pestilence that stalks in the darkness, nor the plague that destroys at midday. A thousand may fall at your side, ten thousand at your right hand, but it will not come near you. You will only observe with your eyes and see the punishment of the wicked. If you say, "The Lord is my refuge," and you make the Most High your dwelling, no harm will overtake you, no disaster will come near your tent. For he will command his angels concerning you to guard you in all your ways; they will lift you up in their hands, so that you will not strike your foot against a stone. You will tread on the lion and the cobra; you will trample the great lion and the serpent. "Because he loves me," says the Lord, "I will rescue him; I will protect him, for he acknowledges my name. He will call on me, and I will answer him; I will be with him in trouble, I will deliver him and honor him. With long life I will satisfy him and show him my salvation."

- **Psalm 23:3,** "He refreshes my soul, He guides me along the right paths for His name's sake."

- **Psalm 51:12,** "Restore to me the joy of your salvation and grant me a willing spirit, to sustain me."

- **Ecc. 4:12,** "Though one may be overpowered, two can defend themselves. A cord of three strands is not quickly broken."

- **Jeremiah 30:17,** "But I will restore you to health and heal your wounds, declares the Lord"

- **Joel 2:26,** "You will have plenty to eat, until you are full, and you will praise the name of the Lord your God, who has worked wonders for you; never again will my people be shamed."

- **Revelations 21:1-5,** "Then I saw "a new heaven and a new earth," for the first heaven and the first earth had passed away, and there was no longer any sea. I saw the Holy City, the new Jerusalem, coming down out of heaven from God, prepared as a bride beautifully dressed for her husband. And I heard a loud voice from the throne saying, "Look! God's dwelling place is now among the people, and he will dwell with them. They will be his people, and God himself will be with them and be their God. 'He will wipe every tear from their eyes. There will be no more death' or mourning or crying or pain, for the old order of things has passed away."

- **Romans 5:9-10,** "Since we have now been justified by his blood, how much more shall we be saved from God's wrath through him."

Redeemed
Hand out two large nails to each woman with a purple ribbon tied to it.

"The measure of Christ's glory is the difference between what you would be by nature, and what you are because of Christ."

- Jack Miller

We have been purchased!!

It happened when Jesus took our sins upon the wooden cross in His death and resurrection, an exchange for the freedom to live. Forever redeemed. Forever saved from this ugly, fallen world we live in. Three nails and our lives are completely changed. Ever think about what life would be like without the gift of forgiveness and grace? A life without redemption is a life captured in slavery. Christ's blood freed us from the bondage of sin; the cross released us physically from the torment of slavery (our sins) in order to have the ability to reproduce good fruit (works) to glorify Him.

God has a funny way of using our deepest wounds to show His glory to others but more importantly, to show us where our character lacked strength. How has God reconstructed your character and given you redemption through the pain?

Questions for Discussion and Reflection:

- What is the meaning of redemption? What does the Bible say about it?

What Does the Bible Say?

- **Psalm 111:9,** "How can a young person stay on the path of purity? By living according to your word."

- **Galatians 2:20,** "I have been crucified with Christ and I no longer live, but Christ lives in me. The life I now live in the body, I live by faith in the Son of God, who loved me and gave himself for me."

- **Colossians 1:13-14,** "For he has rescued us from the dominion of darkness and brought us into the kingdom of the Son he loves, in home we have redemption, the forgiveness of sins."

- **Psalm 19:14,** "May these words of my mouth and the meditation of my heart, be pleasing in your sight, Lord, my Rock, and my Redeemer."

- **Hebrews 9:14,** "How much more, then, will the blood of Christ, who through the eternal Spirit offered himself unblemished to God, cleanse our consciences from acts that lead to death, so that we may serve the living God!"

- **Revelations 5:12,** " Worthy is the Lamb, who was slain, to receive power and wealth and wisdom and strength and honor and glory and praise!"

- **Titus 2:14**, "Who gave himself for us to redeem us from all wickedness and to purify for himself a people that are his very own, eager to do what is good."

- **Ephesians 1:7,** "In him we have redemption through his blood, the forgiveness of sins, in accordance with the riches of God's grace that he lavished on us with all wisdom and understanding."

"Redeemed women of God have tender merciful hearts, backbones of steel, and hands that are prepared for the fight." - Stasi Eldredge

Joy: choosing to see

When our lives are <u>in line</u> with God's Word, we should be experiencing <u>joy</u> everyday, in many ways. God challenges us to <u>find joy</u> in our trials because He knows that it will build <u>character</u> and make us <u>stronger</u>. We have to work to find it, though, and that requires action!

Over the years, I have seen the devil rip marriages apart and cause dissension in the church from the temptations of the world and consequences that follow. I've witnessed people choosing bitterness instead of forgiveness, and then realizing that the grass is not greener on the other side. I've seen a well of emotions reappear after 35 years of betrayal and the pain, caused by the lack of grace given. Generations suffer from selfish decisions and buried joy because facing the truth is just too hard. The devil is having a party as he brings chaos to our marriages and casts a sky of despair over those too weak to fight the battle.

In the Old Testament we see that joy was associated with true worship of God. During King Hezekiah's reign, the Israelites rededicated themselves to God and we read that the people renewed their commitment to God which ultimately reignited the joy in their hearts. Paul experienced joy by simply doing God's will in his ministry and encourages us to find joy in Christ's sufferings. James tells us to "count it all joy" when we are facing trials or in the midst of suffering. The only thing that can steal our joy is sin. By encompassing your life with His Word and His truth, you protect yourself against the flaming arrows that want to rip away your hard earned smile, destroy the baby steps made towards your healing, and reduce the joy that is promised to you through Christ. Allow the joy to shine through to the outside and let others see the beauty in the ashes as God restores your heart and heals your wounds.

Leader Sharing: *Taking Care of the "Me" In Mommy* by Lisa Whelchel says this about praise:

"When we remember His awesomeness, our challenges look smaller in comparison to His greatness. Praise is often the last thing we feel like doing when we need it most. Maybe that is why it is often referred to as a "sacrifice." Hebrews 13:15 says, "With Jesus' help, let us continually offer our sacrifice of praise to God by proclaiming the glory of His name" (NLT). Praise isn't optional - something we can treat as a "luxury" to "pamper" God or ourselves with once in a while "when we have time." Worship (like prayer) is powerful in spiritual warfare; it's a necessary and vital part of protecting ourselves and our children from the enemy. Praise has great power in fighting spiritual battles." [25]

Questions for Discussion and Reflection:

- In Isaiah 55:12, we are told to "go out with joy and be led forth in peace." Have you been able to follow through with that command as you face personal struggles and hardships?

- What things bring you joy from sunrise to sunset?

Leader Suggestions for discussion starter: kids, coffee, deer, hummingbirds, the mountains, the crash of a wave, sunshine, flowers, running, crafts, family, music, smiles, brownies, and knowing God loves me

What Does the Bible Say?

- **Ecclesiastes 7:14,** "When times are good, be happy; but when times are bad, consider: God has made the one as well as the other."

- **Philippians 4:4-7,** "Rejoice in the Lord always, I will say it again: Rejoice! Let your gentleness be evident to all. The Lord is near. Do not be anxious about anything, but in everything by prayer and petition, with thanksgiving, present your requests to God. And the peace of God, which transcends all understanding, will guard your hearts and your minds in Christ Jesus."

- **Romans 12:12,** "Be joyful in hope, patient in affliction, faithful in prayer."

- **James 1:2-3,** "Consider it pure joy, my brothers and sisters, whenever you face trials of many kinds, because you know that the testing of your faith produces perseverance."

- **Galatians 5:22,** "But the fruit of the Spirit is love, joy, peace, forbearance, kindness, goodness, faithfulness, gentleness, and self control."

- **Psalm 16:9,** "Therefore my heart is glad and my tongue rejoices; my body will also rest secure."

- **Psalm 71:23,** "My lips will shout for joy, when I sing praise to you - I whom you have delivered."

- **Psalm 126:5,** "Those who sow with tears, will reap with songs of joy."

"Fear & doubt are conquered by a faith that rejoices. And faith can rejoice because the promises of God are as certain as God Himself."
-Kay Arthur

Boundaries: we all need them

"I once heard that the Greek term for "weaker partner" can also be translated "fine china," which I think is a better translation within the context of marriage. How do you handle fine china? With respect, as you tenderly appreciate and display its finest points. You don't slam fine china around or put it through the blast of a dishwasher."

Fred & Brenda Stoeker

Every Heart Restored [26]

Boundaries are not meant to be boring, make you feel boxed in or caged, or even meant to isolate you from those in your daily life. Boundaries are meant to protect, guide and give others a gauge of what, where and who you are willing to enjoy life with. If we don't have any boundaries, we allow ourselves to be tossed around and become hurt in the process.

Communicating our boundaries with our loved ones is vital to the success of our relationships. Telling those closest to you "that's not okay," or "I'm not going there as it will cause me to stumble," is key to later conversations and consequences. In marriages, having healthy boundaries is like taking a daily vitamin to keep your body strong and in balance. Just like we handle fine china, we need to handle our relationships with care. Some of us may need more boundaries than others; THAT'S OKAY!

If you come from a background where pornography plagues your mind, you shouldn't be going to a movie, dinner or event that would challenge your eyes and mind. Many couples find staying away from alcohol as a boundary they're not willing to budge on in their home or when out with friends. Some have boundaries with their kids that may differ from other parents, and most of us have those in place due to our childhood. As believers, we have a set of boundaries laid out for us in the Bible that can help us determine what is healthy and what is not as we overcome challenges, fears, and betrayal in our lives. Everyone's WILL look different but are necessary to succeed. (Review Ten Commandments: 1. I am the Lord, your God 2. Thou shall bring no false idols before me 3. Do not take the name of the Lord in vain 4. Remember the Sabbath and keep it holy 5. Honor thy father and thy mother 6. Thou shall not kill/murder 7. Thou shall not commit adultery 8. Thou shall not steal 9. Thou shall not bear false witness against your neighbor 10. Thou shall not covet your neighbor's wife or anything that belongs to your neighbor)

Questions for Discussion and Reflection:

- Do you find it hard to place boundaries in your life and stick to them? Did you have clear boundaries prior to the betrayal in your marriage? (Some couples have drawn up a recovery plan based from the example plan found at *https://puredesire.org/pages/tools*. Other couples have weekly counseling appointments as a couple and individually, daily text or phone call accountability check ins, Celebrate

Recovery meetings weekly and in home boundaries needed to keep on track and away from temptation. Know that intense structure is needed in the beginning and after a while - by that I mean however long it takes, even up to years later - the degree of boundaries eases up.)

- Does your spouse agree to the need to establish boundaries around the areas that caused the betrayal to happen? (A repentant heart is willing to accept and engage in having boundaries. Remember, you can only change yourself so if you are met with resistance focus on what you need pursuing healing and wholeness.)

- Has it been hard to deal with someone who may appear like "fine china"?

What does the Bible Say?

- **Matthew 4:6-7,** "If you are the Son of God," he said, "throw yourself down. For it is written: "He will command his angels concerning you, and they will lift you up in their hands, so that you will not strike your foot against a stone."'

- **Isaiah 58:11,** "The Lord will guide you always; he will satisfy your needs in a sun scorched land and will strengthen your frame. You will be like a well-watered garden, like a spring whose waters never fail."

- **Matthew 5:37,** "All you need to say is simply 'Yes' or 'No'; anything beyond this comes from the evil one."

- **Luke 16:13,** "No one can serve two masters. Either you will hate the one and love the other, or you will be devoted to the one and despise the other. You cannot serve both God and money."

Perspective: Stubbed Toes

"Because we often do not think like Him, and because we do not have His perfect perspective, we often do not exactly know what God is doing. Only in hindsight do we understand what is occurring in our personal life, to the church, or in the world in the outworking of prophecy. So we must trust Him, and in the meantime weigh what is happening and its possible outcome."
John W. Ritenbaugh

One morning as I was opening the blinds and turning the lights on, I clumsily stumbled into the LARGE table that had been sitting in the same place for years. It is beyond frustrating to stub your toe, and unbelievable how something so small can create such pain! I immediately had shooting pain and within an hour a black and purple pinkie toe. As I was icing my "serious" injury, I had an epiphany: Sometimes the pain we encounter due to a ridiculous injury like stubbing our toes, parallels how simple, avoidable sins can affect our daily lives. There are obvious places, triggers, and things in our society and everyday lives that we KNOW will cause pain, but we still run into them and stumble because as humans we are weak and far from perfect.

I love what Beth Moore says, "Measure the size of the obstacle against the size of God." How quickly are we to forget the size of God when placed in a difficult situation? We see the obstacles in front of us, feel the pain from the punches, and experience the emotional grief caused by the sinful actions. In the moment, we focus on the initial pain that has been caused and aren't capable to see past the hurt to the bigger picture of the situation. It's not until we take a step back, that we see how we might have been able to avoid the pain, or see how God was, and has been by our side through every side kick, jab, or punch that came our way.

Whether it be fighting a debilitating health issue, dealing with naughty children, frayed friendships, avoiding addictions, stubbing toes or trying to pick up the pieces of your marriage, let God change your perspective so you can see all the <u>glory</u> in the <u>story</u>.

Leader Suggestion for group activity: Give each person a 3 x 5 note card and have them write betrayal in bold letters center of the notecard. Instruct each person to hold the card in front of their nose and ask if they can read what's on the card. Ask if they can see anything else aside from the card. Are the letters blurry? Can you read the word betrayal? Can they see those sitting next to them or across the room from them? Next have each person hold the card out 6 inches from their nose. Ask if they can read what's on the card and if things look any clearer? Can they see more around them or still just the card? Now have each person hold the card arms length from their nose. What's different? What additional things can they see? Are they able to see more friends and family around them? Is their vision still blurred and obstructed from the notecard? Finally, have each person tape the card to the wall opposite of their seat. Now what do they see? Can they still read the card?

The purpose of this exercise is to show how your perspective during betrayal can be clouded by only seeing the pain it causes. Immediately following the confession or discovery, all you see is the fall out of pain caused by sin. It's hard to see others when you are ambushed with emotions and chaos. Over a few weeks, the shock wears off just enough to see a few close family members and friends. It's still extremely hard to focus on anything other than the pain you're experiencing. Fast forward a few additional months and there is additional clarity and the ability to see around the betrayal. It's still in focus, there is still obstruction to your vision but you are able to have a greater view around the pain.

The end result is this. The betrayal becomes apart of you. It will never 100% leave as triggers bring emotions to the surface, consequences linger and for some, betrayal may lead to divorce. You are always aware of the pain and change betrayal caused, but it no longer is in the way of your vision to the future or controls what you are capable of seeing.

This is how perspective after discovery or confession can feel like when walking this journey.

Questions for Discussion and Reflection:

- Can you relate to the notecard exercise and if so, how much clarity do you have in your journey? How blurry is your "notecard?"

- Has God change your perspective on issues within your marriage? (Are you able to see now how sin entered the relationship and are you able to own 100% of the 1% of fault you had part in? With greater perspective, are you able to see how things begin to unravel with more grace or hatred?

- Have you been able to grow your character when you "stubbed" your toes? (Some women have said they are quicker to forgive and extend grace when confronted by someone else's sin. Before the confession or discovery they held onto "things" much longer than what God instructs them to.)

What does the Bible say?

** I can't forgive myself and those who have hurt me.

- **1 John 1:9,** "If we confess our sins, He is faithful and just and will forgive us our sins and purify us from all unrighteousness."

- **Romans 8:1,** "Therefore, there is now no condemnation for those who are in Christ Jesus."

** I can't keep going. I'm tired.

- **Psalm 91:15,** "He will call on me, and I will answer Him; I will be with him in trouble, I will deliver him and honor him."

- **2 Corinthians 12:9,** "But He said to me, "My grace is sufficient for you, for my power is made perfect in weakness." Therefore I will boast all the more gladly about my weaknesses, so that Christ's power may rest on me."

** I feel so alone.

- **Hebrews 13:5,** "Keep your lives free from the love of money and be content with what you have, because God has said, "Never will I leave you; never will I forsake you."

- **Genesis 2:18,** "The Lord God said, "It is not good for the man to be alone. I will make a helper suitable for him."

** This is too hard to deal with.

- **Philippians 4:13,** "I can do all this through Him who gives me strength."

- **1 Peter 5:7,** "Cast all your anxiety on Him because He cares for you."

- **John 16:33,** "I have told you these things, so that in me you may have peace. In this world you will have trouble. But take heart! I have overcome the world."

** I'm afraid.

- **2 Timothy 1:7,** "For the Spirit God gave us does not make us timid, but gives us power, love and self discipline."

- **Psalm 23:4,** "Even though I walk through the darkest valley, I will fear no evil, for You are with me; Your rod and Your staff, they comfort me."

Dating: creating the new "us"

In the beginning of our time together, we talked about grieving over the death of your marriage. We've walked through the emotions of betrayal and discussed ways to protect against further confessions. It's almost impossible to not think about the person who sinned against us, but we've challenged each other to keep the focus on our own hearts. We've invited forgiveness into our lives as we seek more depth to our healing journeys, praying God would reveal the dark places in our lives that needed His mercy.

Now it's time to dance.

The dance you and your spouse were doing before led to destructive behaviors. Finding a new dance can be terrifying, exhausting and requires some level of trust that may not be existent yet. But, I want to encourage you to try! Start small and give yourself room to stumble.

Tim and I started dating each other again after the days of separation and beyond. At first it was all I could handle to just have him sitting on the couch across from me. That soon changed and we found ourselves at a coffee shop, then dinner. We had to start all over again, but it was worth every new move and twirl in our marriage to get to where we are today. Yes, there will be setbacks, discouraging conversations or painful counseling appointments you sit through, but the risk is worth the reward.

I can't promise you your marriage will end with happy ever afters. I can't promise you that there won't be more pain and struggle. God tells us in John 16:33 that, "In this world you will have trouble. But take heart! I have overcome the world." The purpose of this course was to reclaim our hearts back to God and to give Him all the glory for our story. If you find yourself in a place with a new sense of peace and clarity, a place where your identity and image is seen through the eyes of Christ, then our time together served it's purpose.

My husband and I are still working on our new dance moves. We don't get it right all the time, but there is a new desire and urgency to serve each other well through our marriage. Creating a new us has been filled with great rewards. If there was anything second to that, it would be the revelation in my own heart of how much my God loves me, cherishes me and wants His best for my life.

Its time for a new dance...what is it going to look like?

Date Night Ideas:
(think of this as self care activities)

- Go ice skating, roller skating, or play a round of miniature golf
- Go on a scavenger hunt

- Go to the park and swING!
- Find a worship service or concert to attend
- Find a coffee house and play board games
- Find a place to volunteer your time to bless others in need
- Take an exercise class together
- Look through old photo albums together
- Set a candle light dinner/picnic and have the kids be your waiters/waitresses
- Go on a photo date! Snap pictures around town then develop them to create a day date photo album
- Walk the mall. Goal is not to buy but to test perfume and cologne along the way
- Re-live a date before you were married starting with the first place you went out for dinner
- Steal the kids' toys and fly a kite!

Questions for Discussion and Reflection:

- What are some other encouraging, interactive date night ideas?

Exercise: Create a date! In past small groups, Stephanie has handed out adult coloring books. The Five Love Languages has a coloring book with scripture verses and prompting questions that works as a great tool for couples. Suggest taking a blanket, packing a picnic basket with treats and water, a potential sunset and box of colored pens, markers or crayons to create a simple and cheap date. (The living room floor or parked car work as well.)

If you find yourself separated or divorced, use this exercise to build in self care. This is more about taking the time to relearn how to laugh and play when your focus has mainly been on recovery.

Suggested Book Resources

- Hope For The Separated *by Gary Chapman*
- The Bondage Breaker *by Neil T. Anderson*
- Every Heart Restored *by Fred & Brenda Stoeker*
- Every Man's Battle *by Steven Arterburn & Fred Stoeker*
- Every Woman's Battle *by Shannon Ethridge*
- Through A Man's Eyes *by Shaunti Feldhahn*
- Swipe Right *by Levi Lusko*
- Sex, Jesus, And the Conversations The Church Forgot *by Mo Isom*
- A Marriage Without Regrets *by Kay Arthur* (study guide available)
- How We Love *by Milan & Kay Yerkovich*
- The Five Love Languages *by Gary Chapman*
- Love & Respect *by Dr. Emerson Eggerichs* (study guide available)
- Desperate Marriages *by Gary Chapman*
- One More Try *by Gary Chapman*
- Sacred Marriage *by Gary Thomas*
- Boundaries In Marriage *by Henry Cloud & Dr. John Townsend*
- The Love Dare *by Alex Kendrick*
- Lies Women Believe *by Nancy Leigh DeMoss*
- Crazy Love *by Francis Chan*
- When His Secret Sin Breaks Your Heart *by Kathy Gallagher*
- Intimate Deception *by Dr. Sherri Keffer*
- Codependent No More *by Melody Beattie*
- Beauty Marks *by Linda Barriack*
- Men Are From Mars, Women Are From Venus *by John Gray*
- The Emotionally Destructive Marriage *by Leslie Vernick*
- Laugh Your Way To A Better Marriage *by Mark Gungor* (DVD series available)
- Broken & Redeemed: A Study On The God Who Redeems Our Stories *by A Love God Greatly Journal*
- One Year Devotions For Couples *by David & Teresa Ferguson*

Online Resources

- Healing Hearts Ministry: The Hem of His Garment Bible Study www.healinghearts.org
- Marriage Teams: Empowering Couples for Winning Marriages www.marriageteam.org

Fill In the Blank Answer Key

Betrayal: weakest, rely, past, closer, heat

Bitterness: heat, consequences

Shame: decision, regret

Grief: permission,

      1. shock & denial

      2. pain & guilt, disappointment

      3. anger

      4. bargaining

      5. depression & sorrow

      6. testing & reconstruction

      7. acceptance

Weariness: acknowledge, strength, grace, you, you

Image: who you, individual, together, identity, consequences, found, Savior

Forgiveness: died, forgave, gave, need, revisit

Hope: verb, best, purpose

Trust: protect, necessary

Education: understanding, educated, roommates, installing firewalls, viruses

Communication: transparent, express, rediscover

Joy: in line, joy, find joy, character, stronger

Perspective: glory, story

Email Templates

Sending an email before a meeting or after is not required, but it allows those attending the small group to feel connected to their leader. The email prior to meeting usually has a snap shot into someone's journey followed with some scripture verses and a question or two to get their minds engaged into the topic you'll be discussing that evening or the next.

The emails sent the day after a meeting have a small review about what was discussed, the blanks in order as they appear according to the topic discussed and the prayer requests mentioned during your meeting.

Below are a few examples of what has been sent for both pre-meeting and post-meeting emails. Feel free to copy and use any of the below material, or create your own!!

• Week One Pre-Email

Subject: The Initial Shock & Betrayal
Time: Monday, 6:30pm
Location: Life Changers Front Room (Westside of the church building)

I am excited to see God move in our hearts and minds as we seek His healing through Reclaimed! Know that myself and others will, and are, praying for you as we talk about some of the deepest hurts in our lives.

We are just a day away from beginning our study on finding hope in the midst of betrayal. I wanted to give you a heads up, and will continue to do so prior to each week, on the topic that will be discussed. Included will be a glimpse into women's journals, a few discussion questions and scriptures to review. Start thinking about the topic and review the questions and scriptures to prepare your heart for the group.

It has been 9 years since that fateful evening of confession in my marriage. God has been so good and has done miracles in my marriage. I'm still on a path of healing and may not have all the answers, but do know that we serve a God who loves us, who desires us to find healing and wants to bless us with JOY! This study was born out of a story of hope and restoration.

Praying God will fill the voids in your life and you will feel His love in your heart!

An excerpt from "a broken wife's journal"....

"Something inside me immediately died. I could not believe what I just heard. This could not be real. I thought I had married a believer!! After all, he went to a Christian school, grew up in a CRC church, and professed to be a believer!! Who was THIS person? How could this be?? I had chosen all the right qualifications in a partner!! You see, I had grown up in an environment where affairs and divorces simply did not happen. My family put Christ at the head of all that we did, and Satan stayed away!! I didn't have the background or landscape of this environment to even imagine it could happen.

His words completely leveled me.

But somehow, I needed to be at my new job in an hour, so I numbly went into an 'out of body' experience, and somehow functioned as if nothing had just destroyed my world. No one could know!! I am not sure how I got through that day, but I did. Once I got home, I became sick to my stomach and the migraine hit. All I could do was go to bed and cry out to God....."HOW COULD THIS BE"!! Hadn't I been doing all the right things for YOU, my husband, my children, living my life for YOU!! We had the marriage I thought my husband wanted, trying to please him in every way. Never would I have suspected this. How could I have missed it? I felt like such a fool. How could I be so stupid? Whats wrong with me?

I felt so degraded, and even embarrassed! I must really be an awful, terrible, unattractive woman that he would want to leave me. The ugly negative humiliating feelings bombarded me and refused to stop. I would never be happy again. My marriage as I knew it was violated and over, and what was once ours, was no longer."

Discussion Questions to prepare to discuss at this week's group:

- When you are faced with a trigger, how do you respond and communicate your worries with your spouse?
- When you reflect back to the raw moments in the betrayal of your vow, what are some of the emotions, the feelings you experienced?
- Have you shared your story with anyone? What prevents you from sharing?

Scriptures to review prior to this week's group:

- Romans 12:17-21
- John 18
- Proverbs 14:10
- 1 John 1:9
- Genesis 3:10
- Psalm 34:4-5

Blessings,

• Week Two Pre-Email

Subject: Navigating Grief & Exhaustion

Date & Time:

Location:

"I'm not sure what I feel right now. I have so many things racing through my mind that it's totally exhausting. Not to mention having to be quick on my feet with answering to a 4 year old who is piecing things together. I have so many questions that I want to ask and things that I want to say but how to say them I'm not sure. I absolutely hate this. I hate that I can't talk to my best friend. I check my email wishing to see your name and then realize that it won't happen. I want to call you to tell you something about the kids but I don't feel right to do so."

- Stephanie's Journal

Discussion Questions to prepare to discuss at this week's group:

• How can we grieve for others without showing guilt for their sins?

• Do you carve out time each day to spend with God?

• Where or what do you find your identity to be rooted in?

Scriptures to review prior to this week's group:

• Isaiah 43:2

• Matthew 5:4

• 1 Peter 5:7

• Revelation 21:4

• Philippians 3:20

Blessings,

Stephanie Broersma

www.reclaimedministry.com

• Week Three Pre-Email

Subject: Shame & Image

Date & Time:

Location:

"The water was boiling hot; my body was numb. There wasn't enough soap to wash the filth, the shame, and feeling of being violated off my skin. By the time I was done rinsing the confession off my body, the shame had scrubbed my skin raw and was now bleeding. My entire being felt raped of everything I knew. The shame of all the events was overwhelming and embarrassing to face not only for myself, but having to bring this forward to family. The first time back in church, I thought all eyes were staring at me because they had somehow heard of the disgusting truth exposed in our marriage.

I felt like I was carrying the shame of not only my husband's secret sins, but also the shame for our kids, our families and our friends who were dragged into our mess.

Through the process of confession, the burden was transferred to me, and along with that came the feeling of shame. I felt guilty for not seeing the sin rooting itself in my husbands life and regret so many movies watched, places visited, or jokes shared. It (betrayal) radically changes you and your perspective.

I find it interesting now that my level of grace has extended miles after walking through my dark valley. It saddens me that I never thought to view adultery through the eyes of forgiveness; rather just anger and hatred. Same with shame. I see hurting people rather than the blanket of embarrassment and the ugliness of the sin around them."

"I find it interesting that my level of grace has extended miles now after walking through my dark valley. It saddens me that I never thought to view adultery through the eyes of forgiveness; rather just anger and hatred. Same with shame. I see hurting people rather than the blanket of embarrassment and the ugliness of the sin around them."

- Stephanie's journal

Webster's Dictionary defines shame like this: shame **noun** : a feeling of guilt, regret, or sadness that you have because you know you have done something wrong: ability to feel guilt, regret, or embarrassment: dishonor or disgrace

• How do you communicate shame? Silent treatment, cold shoulder, retaliation through negative actions, isolation?

If you have a few minutes, Brene Brown has an interesting perspective on shame that I found enlightening. https://www.ted.com/talks/brene_brown_listening_to_shame#t-1218885

"Instead of their shame my people will receive a double portion, and instead of disgrace they will rejoice in their inheritance; and so they will inherit a double portion in their land, and everlasting joy will be theirs."

Isaiah 61:7

Blessings,

Stephanie Broersma

www.reclaimedministry.com

• Week Four Pre-Email

Subject: The Choice to Forgive

Date & Time:

Location:

An excerpt from "a broken wife's journal"....

"Does that mean it doesn't hurt anymore? No. I have to fight those feelings, sometimes on a daily basis. Forgiveness finally became the easy part, because I realized (over time) that I could forgive, because Christ has forgiven me of all my ugliness. Who was I not to forgive. But the forgetting is the difficult part. The ugly memories try to reappear and control my mind and keep me a prisoner. But that just holds me back from the joy that God has for me. I have to consciously wipe the ugliness from my thoughts, even though this wasn't MY sin and guilt to be forgiven, it turned out to be OUR problem. God continues to help me let go of the hurt and anger, release the pain through forgiveness, release the resentment, stop the rehearsing of the pain over and over in my mind, stop stewing in my pain and let it go---free it, so I can be healthy and whole.

I realized that forgiving someone doesn't make _him_ right, it makes _me_ free."

Living with unforgiveness is like drinking the poison thinking the other person is going to die.

Discussion Questions to prepare to discuss at this week's group:

• Have there been situations in your life that have caused you to not trust others and your spouse completely?

• Are there areas in your life where forgiveness is needed?

• Do you have a hard time allowing God to bring justice rather than you punish others for the hurt in your life?

Scriptures to review prior to this week's group:

- Matthew 6:15
- James 5:16
- Acts 2:38
- Proverbs 3:5
- Daniel 6:23

Blessings,

Stephanie Broersma

www.reclaimedministry.com

• Week Five Pre-Email

Subject: Educating Our Realities

Date & Time:

Location:

"Last night was almost too much for me. It was so honest, but also very hard for me because as much as I crave your touch, I hate your touch. I needed you to listen to me and see my raw emotions. Thank you for doing that. If there is any hope for us, we need to communicate. I thought about our communications skills on my walk tonight. For so long, I thought you were just not in the talking mood or exhausted from work. I've wanted for so long to be able to talk to you about so many random things. To have a conversation without any end in sight. I started to think I didn't have anything good to say because I got nothing back in response. Looking back, over the past 7 years with the recent discovery, has shed light on why you never wanted to have certain conversations. It would lead to the truth being exposed and for that I hate you. I hate that the sin in your life stole that joy from your wife. I still have so many questions and this will take a long time to process, but I'm thankful for the three hours we did have to talk to each other last night. I'm confused and exhausted with headaches from all the thoughts filtering through my mind. I want change but I'm not sure how fast it can be achieved. I wish someone would just tell me what to do, when to do it, and how to do it. My days start off with, "okay, here I am Lord, get me through the day," but end up with more hurt, grief, and pain. This is so completely exhausting." - Stephanie's Journal

You may have heard this song by Casting Crowns, but if not, see if you can relate to the story that's being sung. Here is the link to watch the music video: https://www.godtube.com/watch/?v=D7DDPGNX

Discussion Questions to prepare to discuss at this week's group:

- How aware are you of the dangers in your home? How are you protecting yourself and your family from the pressure of temptation?
- What are some ways that you have grown deeper in your marriage? If the marriage ended in divorce, what evidence of God's protection was revealed to you in that process?
- Have you been supportive & respectful of your spouse when sharing your story? Do you take measures to protect your spouse, ex-spouse with your children?

Scriptures to review prior to this week's group:

- Proverbs 18:15
- Hebrews 4:12
- James 1:19
- Psalm 19:14

Blessings,

Stephanie Broersma

www.reclaimedministry.com

• Week Six Pre-Email

Subject: A Restored Smile

Date & Time:

Location:

Confession forced us to communicate. At first I started to journal my inner most thoughts and hurts and then found the strength to share them with my husband. I was able to express things in my heart more clearly ever than before. My fears didn't withhold my tongue and my speech was spoken in love. With any addiction of a spouse, a little worry or concern is left behind. I can communicate in love, "How are your eyes? How is your mind? and express my accountability with my spouse rather accuse in hatred. Being able to have transparent communication in your relationship and finding new ways to express your love towards each other will not only build trust but strengthen your vows.

Gary Chapman in his book, *The Five Love Languages*, helps us discover what our love language is and how vital it is to speak each others language in relationships. This has made a world of a difference in the way we communicate now and it also provides accountability to always have our spouses best interest at hand.

Discussion Questions to prepare to discuss at this week's group:
- How has God given you patience to mend and restore what was broken?
- In Isaiah 55:12, we are told to "go out with joy and be led forth in peace." Have you been able to follow through with that command as you face personal struggles and hardships?

Scriptures to review prior to this week's group:
- Galatians 5:22
- Psalm 16:9
- Psalm 71:23
- Psalm 111:9
- Galatians 2:20

Blessings,
Stephanie Broersma
www.reclaimedministry.com

• Week Seven Pre-Email
Subject: Finding Joy With New Boundaries
Date & Time:
Location:

"Everything we did had intentions to make us better, stronger, and willing to expose anything in our relationship that would sour and spoil our future. Tim and I both devoted every evening once the kids were in bed, to read together, talk together, and watch as many marriage podcasts and DVD's as possible. We met with pastoral staff to help direct us to the right people that could assist us in diving deeper into the issues at hand. Tim and I met separately with counselors. We had a team of close friends and family that held us up in prayer, encouraged us, prayed with us, holding no judgment in the process. Restoration has

led us to a new love for one another, a love that is firm in our faith, grounded in the cross, and ready for whatever else comes our way as our hedge around our home is much taller, able to protect from all the flaming arrows the devil has coming our direction."

- Stephanie's testimony

"Because we often do not think like Him, and because we do not have His perfect perspective, we often do not exactly know what God is doing. Only in hindsight do we understand what is occurring in our personal life, to the church, or in the world in the outworking of prophecy. So we must trust Him, and in the meantime weigh what is happening and its possible outcome."

- John W. Ritenbaugh

"She stood in the storm, and when the wind did not blow her way, she adjusted her sails."

- Elizabeth Edwards

Discussion Questions to prepare to discuss at this week's group:

- Have you been able to fully accept the betrayal in your marriage?
- Are you able to find blessings in your day?
- If not, do you see how that has hindered your journey to healing?
- If yes, how have you seen God's hand of grace in the process of acceptance?

Scriptures to review prior to this week's group:

"When times are good, be happy; but when times are bad, consider:

God has made the one as well as the other."

Ecclesiastes 7:14

- Romans 8:1
- Psalm 91:15
- Philippians 4:13
- 1 Peter 5:7
- John 16:33

Blessings,

Stephanie Broersma

www.reclaimedministry.com

• Week Eight Pre-Email

Subject: Perspective Moving Forward

Date & time:

Location:

> "The best we can hope for in this life is a knothole peek at the shining realities ahead. Yet a glimpse is enough. It's enough to convince our hearts that whatever sufferings and sorrows currently assail us aren't worthy of comparison to that which waits over the horizon. "
>
> *- Joni Eareckson Tada*

Discussion Questions to prepare to discuss at this week's group:

- Has God changed your perspective on issues within your marriage? Do you know your "why?" The why things went sour; the why behind the break of vows? You can't fix something if you don't understand how it broken.
- If you were faced with a diving accident and forced to live your life in a wheelchair, would you be able to see through the obstacles as clearly as Joni Eareckson Tada has and use the new surroundings as positively as Joni has?
- What are some encouraging, interactive date night ideas?
- What have you learned about the three trees and how have you changed over the past 8 weeks?

Scriptures to review prior to this week's group:

- Acts 15:32
- Hebrews 10:24
- Galations 6:2
- Romans 15:7

• Example of a Post Meeting Email

(Week One)

Good afternoon Ladies! Thank you so much for stepping out in courage to a group with strangers, sharing your intimate story and being willing to have God show you areas of healing still needing to be cleansed, mended and HEALED! Below are a few highlights not in your notes, as well as our prayer requests.

Here are the fill in the blanks as they come in order under the topic Betrayal: weakest, rely, past, closer, heat

(There is also a cheat sheet in the back of your book with the fill in the blanks.)

"Betrayal puts a fog over your judgement in relationships. It clouds your vision to respond and react in a trusting manor."

"Pride more often than not, is the fuel that starts the flame of an affair."

Deu. 32:15 - Since the nation had received God's revelation and His instruction, it should have become upright. (vs. 4) Instead, the nation would grow fat and rebel. Betrayal comes with consequences.

"Your entire thought process will become distorted and inaccurate when under stress turmoil. Make sure we separate the facts from fantasy."

Prayer Requests:

Sally - pray for her as the triggers become present

Molly - pray as she navigates her work place with the other women present in the office.

Donna - Pray for continued health and physical strength

Emily - Pray for her relationship with her son. God we ask you clear schedules and pre-coincieved ideas of all the why's and who's that has gotten the distance to this extent. Give these two a clear slate and an afternoon of pure joy.

Annamarie - 2 yrs. this week since discovery of her husbands addiction. Pray for her during the anniversary. Also, pray for her husbands workplace to become a safe place around other women and give Annamarie a spirit of calm rather than paranoia.

Stephanie - Tim's quick trip to the pit (Vegas) that God protect his eyes and mind.

(Week Two)

Blessings to you this week! If you feel like you're struggling, shoot me, or all of us, an email so we can pray for you in the moment. If you need an ear to listen, give me a call. There will be stuff that will surface as we dive into the first few weeks of the "heat." Be on the look out for the devils ways of tripping you up. Call out to God! You are all incredibly strong, faithful and BEAUTIFUL women that is now my honor to walk alongside of for these next few weeks.

Here is the link to the article I mentioned about grief affecting us physically. Pretty powerful stuff if you think about how your body suffered directly after discovery or confession. For those that have a trickle of information over many years, this could explain any long-term physical pain. I've seen some women after the divorce is final, physically crumble because their body finally senses safety. God made our bodies so unique and complicated.

http://griefwords.com/index.cgi?action=page&page=articles%2Fhealing_body.html&site_id=2

Fill in the blanks as they appear: (grief) permission, (weariness) acknowledge, strength, grace, you, you
Prayer Requests:

Sally - seeking God's purpose for her life

Molly - seeking God's purpose for her life especially in the work place, thank you that she has joy in her boring day job being able to have more time with her daughter.

Donna - continued health and strength, praise that she doesn't feel guilt or a heart pull when her ex-husband contacts her.

Annemarie - she has 2 job interviews this week, pray hey go well

Emily - wisdom and guidance in how to protect herself and kids, direction in her marriage and calm in the anxiety

Stephanie - pray that Tim and I can enjoy our weekend away.

See you all next week!

Acknowledgements

Reclaimed Small Group Guide was birthed from a multitude of emotional coffee dates with broken women. Women who have experienced similar betrayal as myself and who continue to pursue healing. To God be all the glory in the many stories he continues to mold into greatness. For each hurting wife who trusted me with her story and allowed me to walk alongside her, I thank you.

Tim, my love and my husband. Without your confession, we would not be who we are today. Tim, thank you for your obedience to confess, your willingness to listen to God's voice, your choice to become accountable, and your steady love when I am unlovable. Thank you for loving me during my ugly moments and accepting the space needed to take back our marriage. Thank you for giving me full transparency into your heart and mind so that I could learn to trust and love you more than I ever thought possible. You and me, my love. You are the leader Jesus has always wanted for our family, and I'm truly honored to be your bride.

Pastor Kim and his wife Anne Ryan, thank you for being incredibly bold yet gentle mentors in our lives, both before and after the confession. Your grace and ability to speak truth into my life that first night changed the tone of my marriage.

Mom and Dad, thank you for never judging or pointing fingers when things all fell apart. Your sacrifice to love me unconditionally has been a remarkable example of Christ's love. I will forever appreciate all the moments you held me when weeping or gave me room to process as you graciously cared for our kids. I'm so grateful for your continued active role in their lives. You are my inspiration. I love you both so very much.

Catherine, my friend and sister in Christ, thank you for catching me minutes after Tim's confession, even with all the snot and tears of confusion falling to the floor. Your immediate willingness to hold my hand through such intense moments spoke to me of forgiveness and humility. Thank you for our times in search of God's beauty near your home and for encouraging me to build in self-care. Your prophetic word over my life continues to become reality. I am forever grateful for our friendship.

Pastor Kurt, the support and words of affirmation you have given toward our ministry and our marriage have been exceptionally powerful to both Tim and me. Your honesty, messages of truth and hope, and your friendship are never taken for granted.

Ramona and Michelle, thank you for your constant encouragement and gentle nudge to turn this study into a reality. Your support in the ministry has been unwavering.

And to all our other *family and friends*, thank you for your constant love and forgiveness toward me whether you knew my story or not. To those who cried with me, cheered me with countless hours of support, and prayed quietly when you knew I was weak, thank you.

Notes

1. Catherine Theriault, personal handwritten prayer, "A whisper from God," April 2009.

2. J. Allan Peterson, The Myth of the Greener Grass(Tyndale House Publishers; 1984), 111.

3. Tim Jackson, When A Spouse Is Unfaithful, by Our Daily Bread®, © 1999, 2002 Our Daily Bread Ministries, Grand Rapids, MI. Reprinted by permission. All rights reserved.

4. Nelson's Compact Bible Commentary, 2 Chronicles 26:16.

5. Nelson's Compact Bible Commentary, 126.

6. Nelson's Compact Bible Commentary, 549.

7. Neil T. Anderson, The Bondage Breaker (Harvest House Publishers: 2006), 222-224.

8. Nelson's Compact Bible Commentary, 388.

9. Nelson's Compact Bible Commentary, 433.

10. Christian Jarrett, "Does This Brain Research Prove That Humiliation Is The Most Intense Human Emotion?" May 5, 2014, https://www.wired.com/2014/05/does-this-brain-research-prove-that-humiliation-is-the-most-intense-human-emotion/.

11. Brown, B. (2019). *Listening to shame.* [online] Ted.com. Available at: https://www.ted.com/talks/brene_brown_listening_to_shame [Accessed 1 Jul. 2019].

12. Gary Chapman, Desperate Marriages (Northfield Publishing: 2008), 180-181.

13. https://www.crosswalk.com/faith/bible-study/the-most-frequent-command-in-the-bible.html

14. Alan D. Wolfelt titled, *"Healing Your Grieving Body: Physical Practices for Mourners."*

15. Nelson's Compact Bible Commentary, Nehemiah 9:20.

16. "Who we REALLY are - Our identity in Christ," GreatBibleStudy.com http://www.greatbiblestudy.com/who_we_really_are.php

17. Neil T. Anderson, The Bondage Breaker (Harvest House Publishers:2006).

18. "Trust and Obey" lyrics by John H. Sammis (1846–1919), music by Daniel B. Towner (1850–1919); Public Domain.

19. Leadership Journal, "Leadership Survey."

20. "The Most Viewed Porn Categories Of 2017 Are PRetty Messed Up." Fight the New Drug. https://fightthenewdrug.org/pornhub-reports-most-viewed-porn-of-2017/ (accessed May 21, 2018).

21. Paul M. Barret, "The new republic of porn," Bloomberg Businessweek, June 21, 2012.https://www.bloomberg.com/news/articles/2012-06-21/the-new-republic-of-porn (accessed June7, 2018).

22. Maryam Kamvar and Shumeet Baluja, "A large scale study of wireless search behavior: Google mobile search."
     CHI 06: Proceedings of the SIGCHI Conference on Human Factors in Computing Systems (2006): 701-709. http://
     www.kevinli.net/courses/mobilehci_w2012/papers/googlemobilesearch.pdf (accessed June 7, 2018).

23. *Slow Fade* by Casting Crowns, 2007.

24. Chapman, Gary D., and Ross Campbell. The Five Love Languages of Children. Chicago: Moody Press, 1997.

25. Lisa Whelchel, Taking Care of the "Me" In Mommy (Thomas Nelson Incorporated: 2007) 35.

26. Stephen Arterburn, Fred Stoeker, Brenda Stoeker, Every Heart Restored (WaterBrook press: 2004).

About the Author

Stephanie Broersma is a living example of how God brings beauty from ashes in the lives of His children. Married since 2002, she and her husband, Tim, have walked through the valley of marital betrayal and come out the other side stronger, more in love, and fully devoted to Christ. She now heads Reclaimed Ministry, an organization that seeks to help other broken brides recover from the pain and devastation of marital infidelity.

Visit **www.reclaimedministry.com** to watch the Broersma's testimony videos, and read more about the Reclaimed Ministry.

Photo credit by Jodi Van Straalen and the SNAPsisters Photography. www.thesnapsisters.com

Visit **www.reclaimedministry.com** for more information, to purchase *Reclaimed* products, and to see where a small group meets near you.

Made in the USA
Middletown, DE
13 September 2019